STAFFORDSHIRE
SPANIELS

A Collector's Guide to History, Styles, and Values

Adele Kenny

Schiffer Publishing Ltd

77 Lower Valley Road, Atglen, PA 19310

Published by Schiffer Publishing, Ltd.
77 Lower Valley Road
Atglen, PA 19310
Phone: (610) 593-1777
Fax: (610) 593-2002

Please write for a free catalog.
This book may be purchased from the publisher.
Please include $2.95 for shipping.
Try your bookstore first.

We are interested in hearing from
authors with book ideas on related subjects.

•DEDICATION•

For Yeatsy,
my loyal companion and faithful friend
who teaches me daily,
through unqualified devotion and love,
what the special relationship between dogs and their people
is all about.

•ACKNOWLEDGMENTS•

I would like to extend my sincerest thanks to all of the people who assisted me in the preparation of this book. First, to Adele Petro Kenny, my mother, who has always encouraged and supported my writing and collecting interests; to Bob Fiorellino for his unfailing friendship and for all the hours he spent in photo-taking; to Alex Pinto for his insights, advice, and practical "on-line" assistance; to Dan Vaganek for serving as computer consultant; to Michelle Rowland who proofread the original "Spaniel manuscript;" to Arnold Kowalsky who graciously shared his knowledge of factory marks; to Park Photo in Scotch Plains, New Jersey for their many considerations in photo processing; to Catherine Doty for contributing her artwork; and to Pam Kizmann for her expert and speedy restorations.

Very special thanks go to Anita L. Grashof (without whom this book would never have been written) for introducing me to Staffordshire Spaniels, for generously sharing her abundant professional expertise, for her personal friendship, and for helping me build my collection.

Special thanks also go to Nancy Schiffer and Jeffrey Snyder, my editors, whose patience and professionalism helped make this project the delight I hoped it would be, and to the dealers and collectors who invited me into their shops and homes and who made arrangements for me to photograph their Spaniels at various shows (despite the inconvenience of camera, tripod, backdrops, and lights): Barbara & Melvin Alpren Antiques (West Orange, New Jersey), Marla W. Chaikin (William Charles Antiques, Shrewsbury, New Jersey), June deBang (The Old Forge, Scotch Plains, New Jersey), Patricia Elaine, Director (Morristown Antique Center, Morristown, New Jersey), Jean A. Fromer (South Plainfield, New Jersey), Nancy H. Furey, Joan Gibbs, Anita L. Grashof (Gallerie Ani'tiques, Stage House Village, Scotch Plains, New Jersey), Glenbrook Antiques (Cold Spring, New York), Jane McClafferty (New Canaan, Connecticut), Zane Moss Antiques (New York, New York), Perry Joyce Antiques (Winnetka, Illinois), and David P. Willis (Plainfield, New Jersey).

Photographs by Bob Fiorellino and the author
(unless otherwise noted).

• TABLE OF CONTENTS •

• INTRODUCTION •

Staffordshire Spaniels are colloquially known as Comforter Dogs, and are called synonymously Staffordshire Spaniels, Comforters, Comforter Dogs, and Comforter Spaniels. Typical Comforters were modeled after the King Charles Spaniel, often with stylistic leaps of imagination, but always with a *basic* breed resemblance that makes them all uniquely similar. They all have that well-known Spaniel "personality," from the most primitive samples to the more lavishly molded and decorated. Essential components of the Spaniels' distinctive look are an inverted "smile" and wide, painted eyes. In addition, nearly all Staffordshire Spaniels are characterized by a neck chain, collar, and padlock (sometimes called a locket). They are seen in various sizes, styles, and colors, and are sometimes combined with other figures. Some are portrayed lying down or with brightly colored baskets in their mouths. Best-known, though, are the seated, flat-back Spaniels which were manufactured in pairs, one facing left, the other facing right. In their day, Comforters were not considered fine pottery and were purchased primarily by families of modest means to decorate their hearths and chimneypieces.

Comforter Spaniels are usually collected in pairs, although special single models can be equally desirable. Once plentiful and not highly prized, they are currently known world-wide as a valuable, often pricey, antique collectible. Their value has appreciated considerably since the 1950s and will continue to do so as they become more rare and fewer samples enter the market.

Most Staffordshire Spaniels are correctly called pottery despite the fact that some models have porcelaneous bodies. Different techniques employed by the potters, especially those used in firing, resulted in different production results. Generally speaking, the process for making Comforter Spaniels began with molded clay heated in a kiln to form a pottery product.

This black and white single Spaniel is one of many similarly molded and decorated Spaniels potted during the 1850s. The frequency with which this model is seen in today's market suggests that it was popular among Victorian consumers and thus produced in great quantity. 10.25". Circa 1850. Value: $450.00-$550.00. *Courtesy of Nancy H. Furey.*

These wide-eyed Spaniels possess the animated expression and character which typify classic Comforter style. Many pairs of this kind were produced during the mid-nineteenth century and although their appearance is much the same, subtle differences in size and painted detail are always present because each figure changed hands several times during the potting process. Most of the decorating was done by women and young children. This pair was colored in white and decorated with gold polka dots. Eye and muzzle areas were carefully painted in orange, yellow, and black. 12". Circa 1850. Value: $850.00-$950.00. *Author's Collection.*

Many types of pottery have been produced in Staffordshire since the fourteenth century. During the eighteenth century, portrait figures were manufactured in large quantities, and some dog breeds began to appear. The dog figures, which date from 1720 to 1900, are characterized by a crude beauty, a naivety of design, and a charming simplicity. In terms of production and popularity, Comforter Spaniels became a "pet project" of the potteries from about 1840 through the 1890s. This was Staffordshire's greatest period of production, quality, and consumer interest and was roughly concurrent with Queen Victoria's reign on the British throne (1837-1901). The years of the Comforter are set within a remarkably brief period of Staffordshire pottery history — brief but brilliant — and the Spaniel models it produced are so aesthetically compelling that, for many, to speak of Staffordshire dogs is to speak of Staffordshire Spaniels.

A grouping of similarly molded, but differently colored and detailed, right-sided Spaniels which represent various decades of Spaniel production. Left to right: 13", 13.75", 12.50", 13". Circa 1850, 1870, 1860, 1880-1890. Value: $400.00-$500.00 each. *Author's Collection.*

My interest in Comforter Spaniels began in Anita Grashof's Gallerie Ani'tiques a few days after I adopted a ten-week old Yorkshire Terrier puppy, Yeats. I have always loved Staffordshire china and have collected Flow Blue for many years. The fact that my paternal grandmother's family came from Staffordshire may have set the foundation for what I jokingly call a genetically emotional response to Staffordshire wares. Knowing how much I love Staffordshire china *and* my dog, Anita, who specializes in Staffordshire figures, called my attention to several pairs of Spaniels in her shop. I was immediately captivated by their eyes which seemed to mirror a look of innocence and optimistic expectation my own dogs have expressed. I became a collector when research revealed that many Comforter Spaniels were decorated by young children who worked in the potteries. The children's story touched my heart.

The Victorian Era was a time of domestic and foreign prosperity for Britain, a time of great wealth and great power. Within her national borders, political revision, new mass production techniques, and expanding transportation systems helped fill the Empire's coffers. In addition, colonial holdings across the globe increased revenues and contributed to Britain's dramatic rise to world-prominence in politics, commerce, and finance.

The upper and middle classes were the main beneficiaries of Britain's abundance. The aristocracy grew more affluent and the middle class rose. Middle class husbands were able to support their families through increased work opportunities outside of the home. Wives kept house, raised children, and devoted themselves to the refinement of their class. A social order based on strict moral conduct and elaborate rules of etiquette developed and an array of manuals was published to advise and direct all aspects of Victorian life. The Victorian poor, however, sank deeper into the privation they had always known. In rural areas, poorer families continued in the old model of collective family labor. The urban poor often lived hand-to-mouth, barely subsisting by whatever means their wits and chance might afford. In England's larger cities, significant portions of the populace were homeless, consigned to days on the streets and nights in doorways or in doss houses where a bed could be rented for a few pence. Like the Artful Dodger, poor city children became pickpockets and thieves, and lower class women, married and unmarried alike, frequently turned to prostitution. "Lucky" women and children found employment in sweat-shops and workhouses.

Perhaps the greatest irony of life in Victorian England was that intricate rules of moral and social behavior, an obsession with decoration, and grand events like the Crystal Palace Exhibition of 1851 were juxtaposed to existence in poorhouses, overcrowded prisons and insane asylums, and the horrors of crime best typified by Jack the Ripper's reign of terror in London's East End. Members of the upper and middle classes were aware of the problems that existed for the poor but most were too comfortable in their own growing security to expend much effort on the poors' behalf.

The British Reform Movement did, ultimately, generate better working conditions and new child labor laws, but such reforms did not measurably affect the Staffordshire potteries during the early and middle years of Spaniel production. Child workers in particular were forced into long and arduous labor to help support their families. In books like *Oliver Twist*, Charles Dickens and other Victorian writers underscored their fiction with important social commentary, particularly in regard to the plight of starving children who suffered the indifferences and cruelties of an embellished and commercially-minded age. These were the children who worked in the Staffordshire potteries, children whose only hope against hunger and neglect lay in their ability to work.

Conditions in the potteries were particularly poor. A typical workday began at four or five in the morning and did not end until nine or ten at night. Workers, many as young as seven years old, received as little as one or two shillings per week[1] (twenty shillings equalled £1). An 1842 report, compiled by Samuel Scriven regarding the employment of children in factories, contains an entry which names Richard Moreton, a nine year-old boy, who worked at the Hilditch and Hopwood China Factory in Longton. According to the report, Richard had been working at the factory for about a year and three months, began work at approximately seven o'clock each morning, and returned home at seven or eight at night. He was paid for each piece he produced, and is quoted as stating that he could make up to forty dozen small figures in a day. His wages were about two shillings per week. Richard's situation was somewhat unique because his father owned the factory in which he worked which meant that, unlike most working children, he was, at least, well-fed.[2]

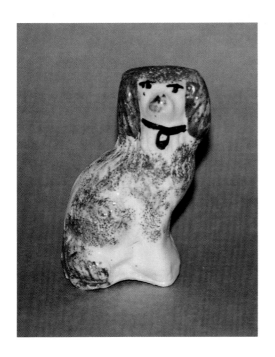

silently speaks of the loyalty and love my "real" dogs have given me. But even more importantly, they remind me of the poor children who labored to decorate them, children who frequently did not outlive their youth, and who spent as many as sixteen hours a day painting the dogs which were, in all probability, the only "pets" they would ever know. Behind every Comforter Spaniel's turned-down mouth I see a lonely child's desire to smile; and in every Comforter's eyes I see a comfortless child's soulful expression, innocent and trusting — half sad and yet half hopeful — an expression which is hauntingly dog-like and human at the same time.

Extremely rare apprentice's model. This small Spaniel was purchased in England and was labeled an apprentice's model. During the nineteenth century, inexperienced workers were required to practice molding and decorating figures, usually after hours, before they were allowed to pot and/or paint for by-the-piece wages. Most practice Spaniels were not saved. Crude molding and naive decorating add to this Spaniel's charm; the background and rarity of the piece add to its value. 5". Circa 1855. Value: $450.00-$500.00. *Courtesy of June deBang, The Old Forge, Scotch Plains, NJ.*

Most pottery wages were earned by the piece, so speed and quantity were more important than quality. Workers were often paid in scrip which could be exchanged for cash only at the local pubs owned, in many cases, by the pottery bosses. Women and young children did most of the laborious and repetitive decorating in an atmosphere where drunkenness was commonplace and the air was filled with silicon dust. Lung problems, among even the youngest workers, were not uncommon. Sanitary conditions were virtually nonexistent; there were no toilet facilities and sewer systems consisted of open cesspools that flooded into the streets and public water supplies. Many of the dog figures were dipped by hand into toxic lead glazes, some of which contained arsenic. Both the lead and the arsenic could be absorbed through the skin with fatal results.[3]

I like to think that most collectors consider their Comforters more than a good investment. I find in my Spaniels an endearing and enduring quality that

A chunky-bodied red and white Spaniel with detailed molding and remarkable painted decoration. Boldly styled, this figure's worldly air and aura of unselfconscious dignity are best expressed in finely delineated facial features. 10.50". Circa 1850. Value: $750.00-$850.00. *Courtesy of Jane McClafferty, New Canaan, CT.*

CHAPTER 1

•*THE HISTORICAL CONTEXT*•

Over the centuries, the relationship between dogs and their owners has evolved and changed. Through antiquity and into the not-so-distant past, dogs provided an inexpensive and sadly expendable form of labor that freed their masters from some of the toils of daily chores. Most dogs were valued for the services they performed, around the farm, in sport, and in ancient times, even in battle. The nobility often kept dogs and some cultures revered certain breeds as religious entities as was the case with Anubis, the Egyptian jackal-god associated with funeral rites, but few were the pampered house pets or the privileged and protected family members they are today.

By virtue of their presence among humankind, and because of their close association with human society and culture, models of dogs appear in the early art of many civilizations. They were widely portrayed in pottery, papyrus, and stone during pharonic times and, as Clive Mason Pope points out, in Chinese pottery as far back as the Han and Tang Dynasties.[1] Early dog models have also been found in the pre-Columbian ruins of Mexico and Peru.[2] It was not until the eighteenth century, however, that recognizable dog breeds were modeled in Europe.

Early in the eighteenth century, selective dog breeding (for the purpose of developing the strongest hunting and sporting qualities) became popular, and various lines came into vogue. This interest was reflected in both the painting and the pottery of the time[3] and signaled the beginning of a slightly changed status for the working dog.

While dogs labored to keep favor with humankind, and despite the emotions and efforts of some few individuals, the preoccupation with dogs as pets was slow to develop. Dogs did, however, make interesting ceramic studies and a few owned by famous persons became subjects for the potter's art.

In the beginning of the eighteenth century, the Meissen Factory in Germany produced a variety of hound statuary, and the Royal Factory at Vincennes was acclaimed for its porcelain representations of Madame de Pompadour's Pug seated on a tasseled cushion. Although Pugs were not widely bred or owned in England, they *had* become a breed of choice in France. The British, inclined to copy continental fashions, responded with a porcelain model of William Hogarth's famous Pug, "Trump," first produced in porcelain by the Chelsea Factory. A variety of Pugs followed, from numerous English factories, which often portrayed the dog in typical Pompadour fashion.[4]

This seated Pug model with black muzzle, red mouth and nostrils, brown ears and paws, and two separately molded front legs was among the many produced in Staffordshire in response to Madame dePompadour's famous Pug. A simple mold design captures the sturdy and vigorous Pug spirit. Like most *Spaniel* figures, it wears a collar and padlock. Once plentifully produced, all Pug figures are considered rare today. 9". Circa 1875. Value: $675.00-$725.00. *Courtesy of Perry Joyce Antiques.*

These extremely rare Pugs are most unusual because they represent puppies rather than adult dogs. Distinguished by inset glass eyes, they are also free-standing. Free-standing dog figures without bases or other support were produced mainly toward the end of the nineteenth century. 5.50". Circa 1880-1885. Value: $1595.00-$1695.00. *Courtesy of Zane Moss Antiques, New York, NY.*

The Derby and the Bow Factories, capitalizing on the English enthusiasm for sport, produced not only Pugs but also a number of gun-dog models. These appeared on oval bases decorated to simulate hunting terrain.[5]

Around 1760, the London Delftware potteries created several models of hounds. These were not particularly life-like and, true to their Dutch inspiration, were painted with blue patches and spots on a white background. Pottery rather than porcelain was the preferred medium.[6]

During the eighteenth century, the Wieldon and Wood families of Burslem were among the first to produce rudimentary but competent dog studies in pottery. Their dogs appeared with green, yellow, brown, and blue glazes and were mostly sporting dogs on raised rectangular bases.[7]

Sporting dogs were represented by a variety of models, among which the Greyhound figured prominently. This outstanding Greyhound with a hare in its mouth is a delicately yet powerfully molded and decorated example of the sporting-dog figures that were popular during the mid-nineteenth century. Separately molded legs, tufts of slip-crafted scrub grass at each paw, a cut-out tail, uniquely molded oval base, and the hare's "pricked-up" ears combine with angular symmetry and balance to define this figure's unquestionable quality. 7.50". Circa 1850. Value: $475.00-$575.00. *Courtesy of Anita L. Grashof, Gallerie Ani'tiques, Scotch Plains, NJ.*

When the process for making bone china was discovered early in the nineteenth century, porcelain factories began to turn out a wider variety of canine figures. Minton produced Spaniels, Greyhounds, and, of course, Pugs. Similar china models were produced at the Alcock Factory and at Derby; Rococo style bases were added in keeping with the taste for ornamentation that characterized designs of the period.[8] But, despite the fact that dogs made interesting and attractive subjects for pottery and china statuary, they were, for the most part, still "blue collar" creatures whose ability to serve humankind was their greatest asset.

A significant change in attitude came about in England during the early years of the nineteenth century and coincided, not by accident, with the manufacture of Staffordshire Spaniels. The Staffordshire Spaniel might even be called a uniquely British symbol of the era in which the dog's station among humankind was elevated from servant to family member.

As is the case with a whole range of items termed "Victorian antiques," a quantity of Staffordshire Spaniels was produced during Queen Victoria's reign as a result of her considerable influence on the cultural and social mores of nineteenth century England. In February of 1833, four years before she acceded to the throne, Victoria adopted a King Charles Spaniel which she named "Dash." Three years after Victoria's coronation, the royal prefix was added to the Society for the Prevention of Cruelty to Animals,[9] which encouraged a respect for animals, dogs in particular, that had existed only to a limited extent under other monarchs.

King Charles Spaniels were all the rage in nineteenth century Britain. When Victoria, beloved queen of the largest empire in the world, introduced her Spaniel, Dash, to her people, the breed claimed an entire nation's attention. Few were immune to the Spaniel's charm, its sweet disposition, and its loving, lap-dog demeanor. No middle-class home was complete without at least one pair of pottery Spaniels, a Spaniel painting, etching, or engraving, or some other decorative item which spoke of the Spaniel's presence in Victorian Britain. This nineteenth century oil on canvas might well have hung above a mantle, flanked by a Staffordshire Spaniel on each side. *Courtesy of Marla W. Chaikin, William Charles Antiques, Shrewsbury, NJ.*

Gun-dog model which portrays a hunter with a gun and what appears to be a Fox Hound on a simple square base. Gun-dog models were popular among the Staffordshire potters during the eighteenth and nineteenth centuries but were produced in limited quantities after the advent of the Spaniel's popularity. 7.25". Circa 1875-1880. Value: $425.00-$525.00. *Courtesy of Anita L. Grashof, Gallerie Ani'tiques, Scotch Plains, NJ.*

After the new queen married Prince Albert in 1840, the royal family grew to include nine children and several dogs. But Dash remained the queen's favorite pet and constant companion. He was presented to the public not as a servant or sporting dog but, rather, as a cherished member of the British royal family. Symbolically, he sat beside his mistress on the throne. The charming nature of Dash's relationship with the reigning monarch and her family touched the collective British heart, and he was painted and printed extensively, alone, with Queen Victoria, and as an integral element of family groupings. (Most noted among the "Dash paintings" are a portrait of Victoria and Dash by Sir George Hayter, completed when Victoria was sixteen years old, and an 1836 portrait of Dash by Sir Edwin Landseer.)

Because Queen Victoria's Spaniel had become famous, Spaniels were not only potted, but painted, printed, and embroidered as well. The large nineteenth century papier-mâché tray shown here is one of the many Spaniel products that Victorian consumers purchased by the score. *Courtesy of Marla W. Chaikin, William Charles Antiques, Shrewsbury, NJ.*

Victoria's subjects began to project their queen's love for her treasured pet to their own dogs, and pottery dog models reached a height of popularity never before seen. The Staffordshire potters, keenly aware of market potentials, "walked the dog" on a "leash" of national enthusiasm. Pairs of pottery Spaniels attracted consumer interest in particular and became favored mantlepiece ornaments.

Manufactured in a range of sizes and styles, the Spaniels were called Comforters, a term deriving from the time of Elizabeth I when ladies were said to have hidden small Spaniels (then called Spaniells Gentle) under their wide skirts to provide the "comfort" of added warmth during the cold winter months.[10] It is also said that just after Mary Queen of Scots was beheaded, a small black and white Spaniel was found hidden beneath her petticoats. Small Spaniels like these were the prototypes and forerunners of the King Charles Spaniel, ultimately named for King Charles II whose court was metaphorically "littered" with this breed of royal choice. Through the years, King Charles Spaniels underwent numerous changes in appearance and at one point were known as English Toy Spaniels. Today, their original features have been restored and they are currently being bred as the Cavalier King Charles Spaniel.

This "seated Spaniel" is an outstanding example of the Cavalier King Charles Spaniel as it appears today. Cavs, as they are affectionately known, are a twentieth century breed in which the original features of the King Charles Spaniel have been restored. Shown here, in typical seated Comforter fashion, is Blenheim Cavalier puppy Roi L Maiden Voyage. Her owner and breeder is Elaine J. Lessig of Roi L Cavaliers in Greenbrook, New Jersey. *Courtesy of Roi L Cavaliers.*

This "recumbent or lying Spaniel" is a tri-color Cavalier King Charles Spaniel named Salador Celtic Velvet of Roi L. A prizewinner by all standards, this exquisite lady illustrates the elegance, dignity, and charm of the breed that captured the heart of Victorian Britain. Breeder: Sheila Smith. Owner: Elaine J. Lessig. *Courtesy of Roi L Cavaliers, photo by James Meager.*

It is tempting to label this photo "freestanding red and white Spaniel" or "red and white Spaniel with four separately molded legs." Blenheim Cavalier Roi L Showboat, bred and owned by Elaine J. Lessig, is a perfect example of the lively grace, sporting character, and affectionate disposition of the Spaniel from which nineteenth century potters drew their inspiration. Showboat's wide, expressive eyes and long, elegant ears are among the breed characteristics that distinguish Staffordshire Spaniels. *Courtesy of Roi L Cavaliers, photo by James Meager.*

Other breeds were manufactured in Staffordshire: Afghans, Greyhounds, Harriers, Droppers, Poodles, Dalmatians, Foxhounds, Whippets, Irish Setters, Lurchers, Mastiffs, Collies, St. Bernards, and even a Terrier (which is remotely Yorkshire-like with a long coat and upright ears). In addition, a number of figure group models incorporating human and dog designs were produced in some quantity. Seated Comforter Spaniels, however, were, and have again become, the most popular and the most collectible.

A Greyhound quill holder seen with some frequency in today's market. The design shown here was created during the 1860s; the figure illustrated was produced during the early twentieth century, possibly from a nineteenth century mold. 3.50" (height), 4.75" (length). Circa 1900-1920. Value: $250.00-$300.00. *Courtesy of Anita L. Grashof, Gallerie Ani'tiques, Scotch Plains, NJ.*

A rare miniature red and white Terrier modeled in the style of traditional Staffordshire Spaniels. Its upright ears and distinguishing beard are very like those of today's Yorkshire Terrier. 4". Circa 1850-1855. Value: $375.00-$475.00. *Author's Collection.*

Poodles, in a wide range of styles and sizes, were popular contemporaries of Comforter Spaniels. Today they are eagerly sought by many collectors and are frequently seen on the market. Like Spaniels, Poodle figures have been widely reproduced, but unlike Spaniels, Poodles did not in their day, nor do they now, enjoy the heights of favor reached by Spaniels. Back row: 10"; circa 1875; $850.00-$950.00 for the pair. Center: 7.25"; circa 1900; $200.00-$275.00. Front row: 4.50"; circa 1920; $275.00-$350.00 for the pair. *Courtesy of Anita L. Grashof, Gallerie Ani'tiques, Scotch Plains, NJ.*

CHAPTER 2

•THE STAFFORDSHIRE POTTERIES•

"Staffordshire Potteries" is a generic term that applies to a large number of independently owned factories located in the northern part of Staffordshire County, about 150 miles northwest of London. Pottery-making is a centuries-old industry in Staffordshire and has continued into the present century. Today, Staffordshire pottery products are known and treasured throughout the "collecting" world.

After years of discussion and planning, it was determined in 1910 that the six main towns (Burslem, Fenton, Tunstall, Longton, Hanley and Shelton, and Stoke) should be consolidated into a single county borough, the present-day city of Stoke-on-Trent.[1]

The Staffordshire district was, from the first, ideally suited to the potter's art because it is rich in clay and coal. Lead, another necessary resource, was easily obtained from areas like Lawton Park, six miles to the north.[2]

The Staffordshire potteries have been located for centuries in the northern part of Staffordshire County, about 150 miles northwest of London. *Courtesy of Catherine Doty.*

North Staffordshire was originally a thirty-square-mile tract of moorland comprised of several villages, most of which were involved in the potting industry. By 1800, nearly all the villages had grown into towns. Because the towns shared a common trade, it came to be felt that the interests of local government might best be served through incorporation of the towns.

This nineteenth century horse brass showing a Staffordshire kiln is a mute but clear testimonial to the fame of the "The Potteries." *Author's Collection.*

Throughout the fourteenth and fifteenth centuries, monks in the British abbeys produced quantities of pottery. By the sixteenth century, there were many abbeys in or near Burslem, which eventually became the "heart" of the Staffordshire potteries. During the 1530s, Henry VIII closed England's monasteries, including those in Staffordshire. Their dissolution, however, did little to change the course of British pottery; in fact, it may have opened the field.[3] The potter's craft, which had been monopolized by the monks in England, was ultimately assumed and expanded by laymen helpers whom the monks had taught.

When the monasteries closed, laymen potters continued to produce crude wares in their homes for local use until 1600 when the crown lands in Burslem and Tunstall were divided into copyholds and given to the holders. The land plots were small and, although they were adequate for basic subsistence farming, they were unsuited to more profitable, wide-scale agriculture or livestock breeding. They were, however, perfect for the potters. A newfound security and freedom, combined with available natural resources, afforded the potters an opportunity to establish a growing cottage industry which would one day become world-known.[4]

Most of the potters worked with their families in sheds adjacent to their homes, and many dug their own clay and coal.[5] Pottery-making had to be balanced with attention to farm and household chores. It is commonly understood that while members of individual families shared in the production of pottery, pottery families did not work cooperatively with other families; each conducted its own business. The wares, however, *were* marketed collectively. A scarcity of marked pieces indicates that the early potters saw little need to identify their products with personalized marks. With Staffordshire figures, this practice continued into the 19th century. Accordingly, the Comforter Spaniels collected today carry little notice of their "pedigree."

Around 1690, the Elers brothers, John and David, arrived from Holland to work in Burslem, bringing with them the secret of off-salt glazing used to make a durable, high-quality product called stoneware.[6] The Elers brothers' techniques were copied by the Staffordshire potters and, by 1693, Aaron Wedgwood is known to have produced stoneware of considerable merit.

Pair of extremely rare, white and gilt, salt-glazed seated Spaniels with sgraffito eyes and muzzles. Salt-glazing, as in this example, results in a rough surface texture which is similar to that of an orange skin. 10" (left), 10.50" (right). Circa 1825-1835. Value: $1500.00-$1800.00. *Courtesy of Anita L. Grashof, Gallerie Ani'tiques, Scotch Plains, NJ.*

A legend concerning the Elers brothers' process names one Astbury of Stelton, an Elers employee, who discovered their glazing secret by pretending to be mentally deficient and thus gaining access to workrooms and files that were off-limits to other workers. Astbury is reported to have learned the off-salt formula and then to have gone into business for himself.[7] Widespread production of stoneware by numerous potteries would indicate that equally inventive spies must have been at work throughout the district.

As consumer demand increased, pottery methods became more and more sophisticated, and commonly shared techniques gave way to a variety of undisclosed recipes for molding, mixing, and glazing. A more competitive spirit began to grow among the potters, and successful formulas became carefully guarded secrets. "Industrial espionage" and "pottery plagiarism" were standard operating procedures.

Between 1720 and 1740, Thomas Astbury added calcined flints and white clay from Devonshire to produce the first cream-colored earthenware or creamware. At Tunstall, in 1740, Enoch Booth developed a fluid glaze that enhanced creamware production; and between 1740 and 1760, Josiah Wedgwood further developed and refined the product. The quality of Wedgwood's creamware gained him royal favor and the term "Queensware" was applied to the popular ivory-colored wares he produced.[8]

Early in the 1730s, the Staffordshire potters began to bring alabaster from Derby for use in making molds. Blocks of stone were cut or carved into patterns from which clay molds were made. Fifteen years later, in 1745, Ralph Daniel brought the formula for plaster of Paris from France to England.[9] Mold-casting in plaster offered the Staffordshire potters a cost-efficient and time-saving alternative to block-cutting and provided them with an answer to the demand for greater quantities of more refined wares.

Changes in production techniques, and other developments in methods, brought about the dramatic shift from a simple cottage industry to a thriving factory business in Staffordshire. In 1743, Thomas and John Wedgwood owned five ovens, and a letter written by Josiah Wedgwood in 1762 mentions that there were five hundred potteries employing more than seven thousand workers in the Burslem area.[10]

The Mercy and Trent Canal, completed late in the 1700s, made transportation of Staffordshire pottery quicker and much less expensive.[11] Prior to the Canal's completion, traveling peddlers or crate-men sold Staffordshire figures from door to door in villages throughout England. The potters also offered their wares for sale at county fairs, outdoor markets, local shops, and in market stalls located near theaters or anywhere else the buying public might gather.[12] In terms of long distance marketing, a greater volume of wares could be moved, via the Canal, from Staffordshire to Liverpool for one-seventh of the cost incurred through earlier land and river transport. As a result, market geographies widened and, by the end of the nineteenth century, the Staffordshire potteries had become one of the largest, most productive, and lucrative industries in Britain.[13]

THE FIGURE MERCHANT.
Printed in Colors for God. za Ladys Book by Wagner & M'Guigan

This nineteenth century print, which appeared in a Godey's Ladys Book, is entitled "The Figure Merchant" and shows a Staffordshire traveling peddler or crateman with a tray of wares. *Author's Collection.*

"The Potteries," as they came to be known, were home to a number of potters and potting families of singular reputation and distinction who potted through the eighteenth and nineteenth centuries. These include the Wood family of Burslem, who intermarried with the Wedgwoods of equal, if not greater, renown; John and Rebecca Lloyd, who created the earliest known portrait figures which can be identified as the work of a particular pottery; William Pratt, who colored and fired his wares before application of the final glaze; John Walton, whose lavish use of *bocage* (or foliage) is a distinguishing feature of his designs; Ralph Salt, whose figures sometimes appear with names on a back shield; Sampson Smith of Longton, one of the most prolific Staffordshire potters, who marked some of his figures, including Comforter Spaniels; and Obadiah Sheratt, whose large, complex pieces are considered the true prototypes of Victorian pottery.

Other potters and potteries of note are: H. Bently of Hanley; Ridgway & Robey of Hanley; the Rockingham Factory; the Alpha and Tallis Factories (identified by Balston); Minton of Stoke-on-Trent; John Carr who was either a potter or designer and possibly of Northumberland; George Baguley of Hanley; Kent & Parr of Burslem; Lancaster & Sons, Ltd. of Hanley; James Sadler & Sons, Ltd. of Burslem; and Joseph Unwin & Co. of Longton.[14] There are, of course, scores of others; however, with the exception of the Lloyd and Smith potteries, factory marks were rarely used. While certain figures and Spaniels may be attributed to specific potteries by virtue of stylistic features, potter anonymity has been well-preserved.[15]

The earliest pieces produced in the Staffordshire potteries were portrait and animal figures, models of buildings, inkwells, quill holders, spill vases, and a variety of miscellaneous items. Many were representations of famous persons as well as historical, mythical, theatrical, and literary characters. Most were molded and decorated in a primitive style that is appealingly naive. Pieces produced from around 1840 until 1880, while still characterized by the "hallmark" of Staffordshire simplicity, demonstrated greater attention to detail and were more finely molded and decorated.

All Staffordshire figures share a homely, but popular, rural craft history and, as such, they represent an aspect of British folk art. While the Bow and Chelsea factories drew their inspiration from European models and looked toward a wealthy clientele, the Staffordshire potters drew upon the things they knew best: the details of everyday English life, the royal family, famous persons, authors and literary characters, lithographs, paintings, engravings, menageries of wildlife, *and* the all-time favorite — dogs.

The portrait figure shown here is typical of many produced during Queen Victoria's reign. The potters paid particular attention to members of the royal family and special events in their lives. This figure represents the Price of Wales and Princess Alexandra and was probably issued in or around September of 1862 when the Prince's betrothal to Princess Alexandra was announced. The title appears in raised capitals, painted black, on a white oval base. A taller variation of this figure has been recorded by P. D. Gordon Pugh. 9.50". Circa 1862. Value: $550.00-$650.00. *Courtesy of David P. Willis, Plainfield, NJ.*

Over a period of about two hundred years, millions of figures were produced in the Staffordshire potteries. Their themes and styles number in the thousands, and they range from a few inches to two feet in height. (A twenty-four inch figure of Napoleon is the largest recorded.)[16] The figures came to be known as "image toys" and consumers delighted in them. Similar pieces were potted in factories in Scotland, Wales, and other parts of England but it is likely that at least some of the potters who owned and worked in these factories received their training in Staffordshire. While manufacturers in other parts of the world were producing fine porcelain and china objects, the crude grace of Staffordshire's pottery figures created a category of ornament distinctively its own.

A selection of "image toys" that only hints at the diversity of subjects and styles produced along with Comforter Spaniels in the Staffordshire potteries. *Courtesy of Anita L. Grashof, Gallerie Ani'tiques, Scotch Plains, NJ.*

It is doubtful that the early Staffordshire potters ever realized they were writing one of the most celebrated chapters in potting history, nor is it likely that they considered their work an historical record of their time. Had they understood the significance of what they were doing, their efforts might have become too deliberate and the unpretentious beauty that typifies Staffordshire pottery might have been lost.

Along with increased export markets, the Staffordshire potters exhibited and sold their figures at public sites throughout Britain during the nineteenth century. The old tradition of traveling peddlers who carried trays of figures from village to village continued to some extent but became less and less necessary as improved transportation systems enlarged market geographies. Collectible and pricey today, each image toy sold for a few pennies in its day. *Courtesy of Anita L. Grashof, Gallerie Ani'tiques, Scotch Plains, NJ.*

CHAPTER 3

• MOLDING PROCESSES •

Press-Mold Casting

The earliest Staffordshire figures were modeled entirely by hand in a long and painstaking process. Each model produced, however, was distinctively original. Once mass production was introduced by the mid-1700s, economics held sway and resulted in the use of molds, except in a few rare cases, for Staffordshire figure production.[1]

During the Victorian era, when Spaniel models were one of Staffordshire's best-selling items, molds were used almost exclusively. The process for creating a Spaniel figure began with a sculptor's rendering, prepared by hand in oiled clay. A plaster of Paris mold was made in two or more parts from the sculptor's model. The plaster parts were removed from the sculptor's model to become the master mold. This mold's parts were reassembled, leaving a hollow interior into which more plaster of Paris could be poured to make additional molds. Master molds were usually preserved by the potteries, and some have survived to the present. Working molds made from the master usually produced up to two hundred figures before they had to be replaced.[2]

Most Spaniel molds consisted of two parts, a front and back. Each half was covered with a "bat" (a sheet of wet clay) which was flattened to look like pie crust dough. The bats were then pressed by hand or with a sponge into the sides of the mold parts, leaving the center area open and hollow. (Interior sections of broken Spaniels will sometimes reveal a worker's fingerprints.) The edges were trimmed next, pressed together, and secured with string. The inside seams were brushed with liquid clay through the open bottom. The in-mold figure was then placed on a shelf where it remained until the clay was dry to the touch. When the clay was sufficiently dry, the mold was separated and the figure removed. The open bottom was then covered with another bat of clay and sealed.[3] When the bottom clay was fired, the model was left with a slightly concave base.[4]

This extremely rare Spaniel appears in the biscuit state. Somehow, it "escaped" the potteries before decorating and glazing were begun. A small chip on the figure's mouth may have resulted in "reject" status. Possibly, a pottery worker took the unfinished figure home and it has survived in its early stage of production. 10.25". Circa 1865. Value: $595.00-$695.00. *Author's Collection.*

Back view of the undecorated, unglazed Spaniel. The flat-back surface has been handsomely molded. *Author's Collection.*

Bottom view of the unfinished Spaniel which shows that a bat of clay had been placed on the bottom of the figure. Smooth seams indicate that a repairer had at least begun his work. Had the piece been glazed and fired, the bottom would have become slightly concave. *Author's Collection.*

Back view of a Spaniel showing typical release hole placement near the shoulder on the back of a figure. *Author's Collection.*

When the foregoing process was completed, a "repairer" scraped off any seams left by the mold, and repaired cracks or recessed areas by filling them in with clay or by dabbing on slip (a mixture of clay and water used in decorating, as a cement, or in slip-casting). Additional parts, made from other molds, were added at this time.[5]

Small holes were then made in the base and/or back of the figure, unless it contained a spill or other natural opening, to allow expanding air and gasses produced during firing a means of escape. These release holes were always small, and figures with holes larger than the diameter of a pencil are usually either very late models or reproductions.[6]

Occasionally, a release hole may be found on the head area of a Spaniel figure, as shown in this illustration. *Author's Collection.*

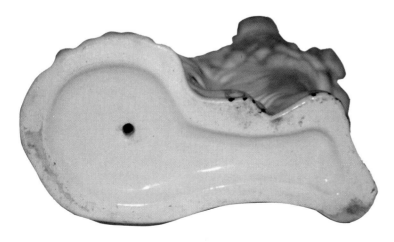

Often, release holes, sometimes called firing holes, were opened in the bases of Spaniel figures, as illustrated in this photograph. *Author's Collection.*

The figure was then fired for the first time at about 1100 degrees centigrade to form a product known as the "biscuit." Hand-painted underglaze color was added and the figure was fired again at 700 degrees centigrade to protect the colors during glazing. The biscuit figure was next dipped into a liquid lead glaze and fired again at 950 degrees centigrade. At this point, the glaze formed a coating over the whole figure. Cooling freshly glazed figures required great care as the glaze needed to cool at the same rate as the body of the figure to prevent shrinking and crazing (small cracks in the glaze) from occurring. Finally, overglaze colors were applied, and the figure was fired for the last time at 800 degrees centigrade in a kiln.[7]

Two-part molds varied only in regard to the features created by the artisan who prepared the original sculptor's model. The front part of a Spaniel mold was usually detailed, but the back was most often flat and either undecorated or sparsely detailed (this because the Spaniel figures were designed to be placed on a mantlepiece or against a wall). A few Spaniels were modeled in the round, and the degree of detail on the front and back differed from figure to figure. Generally, Spaniels produced before 1880 are more finely detailed than those produced closer to the turn of the century. Spaniels intricately detailed in both the front and back are more interesting and more valuable.

Slip-Mold Casting

A method called "slip-casting" was used infrequently during the Victorian era to produce Staffordshire figures, including Spaniels. Slip molds were created in the same manner as press molds. To create a slip-cast pottery figure, a mixture of clay and water (slip) with the consistency of cream was poured into a mold and left to set. The plaster mold, being porous, absorbed the water from the slip. Within a half hour or so, a layer of clay formed against the wall of the mold. The remaining mixture was discarded and the figure was left to dry. When thoroughly dry, the figure was removed from the mold, and the processes for decorating, glazing, and firing were completed according to the same steps used in press-mold casting. Figures made by slip-casting often have open bottoms or large base holes, and the finished products are usually lighter in weight than those that were press-cast.[8]

Nineteenth century potters generally avoided slip-casting because it caused the working molds to wear out more quickly than press-molding did. Most slip-molds deteriorated beyond further use after production of about twenty figures.[9]

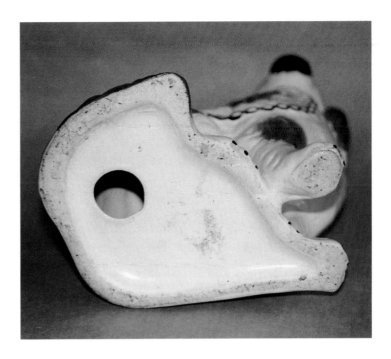

A large base hole is always indicative of the slip-casting method when found on the bottom of a Staffordshire Spaniel. Such holes rarely appear on early Spaniel models and never on figures that were press-cast. *Author's Collection.*

Slip was used by the Staffordshire potters in decorating as well as in slip-casting. To create the curly coat on this Poodle figure and the rough texture on the small pitcher, slip was forced through a sieve and applied to the figures. *Courtesy of Anita L. Grashof, Gallerie Antiques, Scotch Plains, NJ.*

For the obvious reason that more figures could be produced from a single working press mold (without the expense of replacement after manufacture of only twenty or so figures), the potters were not inclined to use the slip-casting method very often. It is seen extensively, however, in twentieth century reproductions and slip-cast Spaniels must be carefully examined to determine their authenticity.

To produce a Spaniel by the press-mold method, a plaster of Pairs mold was made from the mold sculptor's original model. The plaster molds usually consisted of two parts, a front and a back. Sometimes additional molds were required to create special features like separate legs.

Figure A: The plaster mold was separated.

Figure B: Bats, flat sheets of wet clay, were pressed by hand, as indicated by the arrow, into the sides of the mold parts, following the contours of the sculpted design.

Figure C: After the bats were pressed into place, the edges were trimmed, and the mold was pressed together and tied with string. When the clay was dry, the mold was separated again and the hollow Spaniel figure was removed. At this point a repairer smoothed seams, repaired cracks, and opened release holes.

Drawing Courtesy of Antique & Collectors Reproduction News, Box 71174, Des Moines, IA 50325, (515) 270-8994.

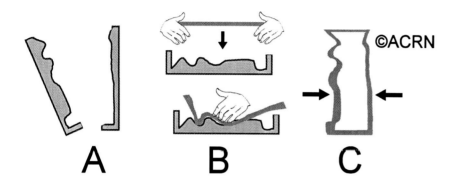

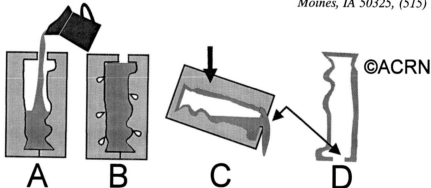

To produce a Spaniel figure by the slip-mold method, the mold was first cast in plaster of Paris in the same manner as a press-mold. However, the mold was not separated and an opening was made in the bottom into which slip could be poured. (In some few cases, the entire bottom was left open.)

Figure A: Slip was poured into a hole in the bottom of the plaster mold.

Figure B: The slip was left inside the mold for a period of time. During that time, the water from the slip was absorbed into the porous walls of the mold.

Figures C & D: A hollow shell formed along the sides of the mold, as indicated by the heavy arrow in C. The remaining slip was poured out, as indicated by the double arrow in C & D (note that slip-cast figures may have one or two holes in the bottom through which the slip was poured in and out). The shell was then removed from the mold.

Drawing Courtesy of Antique & Collectors Reproduction News, Box 71174, Des Moines, IA 50325, (515) 270-8994.

CHAPTER 4

•GLAZING, COLORING, GILDING, AND LUSTERING•

Glazing and Coloring

Although a very few Spaniel pairs were salt-glazed, the majority of early figures were made with color tinted underglazes. This means that most Spaniels received an application of paint before glazing and refiring. Underglaze coloring became popular around the time of Ralph Wood II[1] (1789-85) and appears in most samples of Victorian era dogs. Underglaze colors were varied, and many dog-breed figures appear in bright, natural-looking colors. Comforter Spaniels were most frequently colored in white, black and white, red and white, and, occasionally, in liver and white. Very often, the same Spaniel form was produced with alternative decoration.

Finely painted Comforters with artistic feathering, gilding, and facial details are among the most valuable and collectible Spaniel figures. Some late Spaniels (especially post-1900) were sprayed with color; this effect is easily recognizable and is not usually considered a "plus."[2] Sponged color was applied to some early Spaniel figures but sponged or swabbed decoration has appeared more frequently on modern reproductions.

Unusual apricot coloring on this new Spaniel offers an example of the spray painting technique used on many twentieth century reproductions. The muzzle area lacks detail and shows little evidence of the fine brush strokes associated with hand-painted decoration found on authentic Spaniels. 10". Circa 1920-1950. Value: $225.00-$300.00. *Courtesy of Anita L. Grashof, Gallerie Ani'tiques, Scotch Plains, NJ.*

Painting with sponges was employed only occasionally in the body decoration of early Spaniel figures. The effect could be light and lacy or might resemble the horizontal extensions of stratus clouds. Sponge-painting is achieved by dipping a sponge into paint and pressing it against the body of a ware. Quicker and less-laborious than hand-painting, sponging is often seen on poor quality reproductions but is rarely seen on genuine Victorian Spaniels. 3.50". Circa 1845. Value: $295.00-$395.00. *Author's Collection.*

One popular underglaze color was a rich cobalt blue called Thénard's Blue.[3] Thénard was a French chemist who created the formula for his blue coloring (thirty parts cobalt to one hundred parts alumina) in 1802. After 1863, however, the color seems to have disappeared from use in the potteries.[4] Thénard's Blue was often incorporated into portrait figure designs and is seen on dog model bases. Larger seated Spaniels on cobalt bases are not recorded, but a number of smaller Spaniel figures, and especially Spaniel groupings, appear on oval, square, cushioned, and Rococo blue bases.

The proud red and white parent Spaniel in this figure is presented with a black and white pup on a Thénard's blue base. Both parent and pup have blue eyes, a rarity among all dog-breed models and a feature which makes this figure very collectible. 6.75". Circa 1855. Value: $750.00-$850.00. *Courtesy of Perry Joyce Antiques.*

Overglaze colors (enamels) were sometimes added, as their name suggests, over the glaze. After these enamels were applied, the figures were refired at a low temperature. One problem with enamels was their tendency to fade under the heat of the glost-oven and the requirement of mixing with a vitreous flux. The mixture was then painted on by hand or with transfers or rubber stamps and fired again.[5] The major problem with enamels was that enameled surfaces tended to have a dull, matte finish and a slightly rough tex-

ture. Unlike underglaze colors, enamels often chip or flake. In some portrait figures this is evident in the overglaze black enamel used on hair and shoes;[6] in the case of Comforter Spaniels, chipped or flaked enamels are most noticeable around the eye and muzzle areas.

Overglaze colors, or enamels, were added after a Spaniel figure was glazed. Re-glazing was then required. The main problem with overglaze enamels was that they tended to fade under the heat of the glost oven and mixing with a vitreous flux (glassy glaze) was necessary. Enameled surfaces also tended to have a dull, matte finish and a slightly rough texture. Unlike underglaze colors, overglaze colors often chip or flake and may appear worn on older Spaniels. Note the duller finish and slight flaking on this Spaniel's enameled muzzle. *Author's Collection.*

Gilding

Two types of gilding were used to decorate Staffordshire Spaniels from the earliest figures through the end of the nineteenth century. Identification of gilding types can be helpful in dating, as well as in determining prices.

Although gilding was rarely, if ever, used over *enameled* colors (to avoid the additional firing needed to fix the color)[7], gold was extensively applied over underglazed surfaces, especially on the collars, padlocks, and chains of most Spaniel figures. It was also commonly used in the body decoration of all-white Spaniels to highlight molding details, especially during the later years of production when varied colors were used more judiciously.

The first type of gilding was achieved through

use of a powdered mercuric gold called "best gold." Best gold appears warmly flaxen on finished Spaniels; its effect is light and natural. It must be noted that, after firing, best gold became dull and required burnishing with agate stone or a particular sand,[8] an added chore for the pottery workers. Best gold was the only gilding used on Staffordshire figures until circa 1860 when a product called "bright gold" was introduced. A liquid gilding, bright gold was painted on by brush after the final firing and is easily identified by its brassy, mirror-like shine.

Best gold was used until the end of the nineteenth century but not exclusively after 1860. Bright gold does not appear on any Spaniel figures before that date but was used extensively after 1880 and appears on many reproductions.[9] Despite the fact that best gold is preferred over bright gold among collectors, it is inclined to rub off, especially from the raised areas to which it was applied. Accordingly, Spaniel surfaces gilded with best gold often appear worn. Best gold in good condition, however, is far more appealing and much more realistic than bright gold.

Lustering

Luster has been used to decorate pottery and porcelain for centuries, and metallic luster glazes reached a height of popularity in Staffordshire from about 1775-1830. Even after its peak, luster continued to find favor among consumers and it is still being produced today. Several English factories made copper, silver, and gold lusters during the Victorian period and an iridescent mother-of-pearl was developed in 1860. Luster is rather delicate and can be damaged if rubbed or washed carelessly.[10]

Copper lustered pitcher and copper lustered Spaniel of the same production period. Pitcher: 7". Spaniel: 9". Circa 1885. Value: Pitcher, $100.00-$150.00; Spaniel, $345.00-$445.00. *Courtesy of Anita L. Grashof, Gallerie Ani'tiques, Scotch Plains, NJ.*

Because lustered wares had been popular for some time, it seems only natural that the Staffordshire potters would experiment with luster decoration on Spaniel figures. Most copper lustered Spaniels, of the type shown here, were manufactured during the 1880s and 1890s. Like all Spaniel figures, they were produced in a range of styles and sizes. *Author's Collection.*

A number of lusters appear on Spaniel figures. Copper, gold, and pearly lusters were often used in body decoration or to highlight molding details. Of all, copper lusters, actually made from gold, were used most frequently.

Copper lustered Spaniel with one separately molded front leg (one of a pair). 7". Circa 1880. Value: $375.00-$475.00 (single figure). *Courtesy of David P. Willis, Plainfield, NJ.*

Although Spaniels with copper or gold lustered body decoration are the most commonly seen, other lusters were sometimes sparingly applied to Spaniel figures, especially in the muzzle areas, as shown in this late nineteenth century white and gilt Comforter. *Courtesy of Anita L. Grashof, Gallerie Ani'tiques, Scotch Plains, NJ.*

•TYPES OF STAFFORDSHIRE SPANIELS•

Variant Styles

Comforter Spaniels are most commonly represented by the seated Spaniel. A number of other Comforter figures, however, and Comforters incorporated into groupings, were modeled during the years of Spaniel production. Although these complementary figures are wonderfully engaging, some collectors prefer to specialize and include only seated Spaniels in their collections. For those who choose a more ecumenical approach, it is helpful to learn about the Comforter Spaniel variations that were produced. Because most of the variant styles were not manufactured as abundantly as seated Spaniels were, they are generally more rare and more costly.

Flat-Back Spaniels

While a limited number of Comforter Spaniels were modeled in the round, the greatest majority fit into a category of Staffordshire figures called "flat-backs." Most Spaniels were cast in two-piece molds which included a front section with blocked-in feet and a flat back section designed specifically to be placed against mantle walls.[1] The flat rear area, not designed to be seen, was convenient and safe for display as well as economically advantageous for the potters.

Flat-back surfaces were designed for most Victorian era Staffordshire figures. On these, including the Spaniel figures, the flat areas were simply molded and sparsely decorated. Spaniels presented with great detail on the back are not common and are more collectible and pricey.

Spaniels with Separately Molded Legs

Some Spaniel figures appear with separately molded legs. Supplementary molds were needed to produce this effect of three-dimensional realism. Because the extra molds required additional labor and

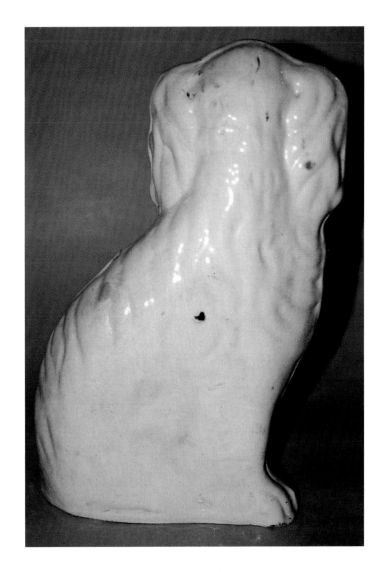

This Spaniel is a good example of the characteristic flat-back chimney ornament produced in Staffordshire. Signs of wear, probably from rubbing against the mantle wall, are evident. Because the backs of the figures were not intended to be seen, most "flat-backs," like the Spaniel shown here, were produced with economy of molded detail and painted decoration. *Author's Collection.*

expense, fewer Spaniels with separate legs were produced in comparison to their solidly molded "relatives." This fact notwithstanding, Spaniels with one separately molded leg are seen with some frequency in today's market. They are, however, more costly to purchase, just as they were in Victorian times. These Spaniels are also more difficult to find in mint or near-mint condition as the legs are more vulnerable to breakage than those that were sturdily blocked-in.[2]

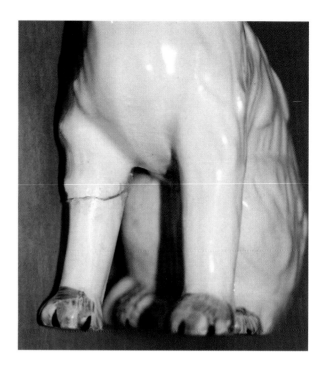

Close-up of the damaged leg on the Spaniel shown in the preceding illustration. The broken leg was simply glued into place by a previous owner. (The good news is that, in the hands of pottery restoration expert Pam Kizmann, the figure was repaired with virtually no visible traces of breakage or repair.) *Author's Collection.*

This little fellow is a sample of the rare models with two separately molded front legs. Regrettably, the right front leg on this Spaniel was broken off, proving the point that separately molded legs are vulnerable to breakage. 6". Circa 1930. Value: $300.00-$375.00. *Author's Collection.*

Spaniels with one separately molded leg are uncommon but available. Spaniels with *two* separately molded legs are quite difficult to find. Both types carry higher price tags than Spaniels with solidly molded legs and, more often than not, the taller the Spaniel, the taller the price.

The Spaniel on the left was molded with one separate front leg in a process that required three mold parts (front, back, and separate leg); the red and white Spaniel in the center was potted in a two-part mold with sturdy blocked-in legs; the Spaniel on the right required four mold parts to create two separate front legs (front, back, right leg, and left leg). *Author's Collection.*

Spaniels on Molded Bases

Many dog-breed figures, and even a number of Comforter Spaniels, appear on molded bases or plinths that were produced in flat, oval, rectangular, square, scrolled, tasseled, or footed forms. Some eighteenth century figures were presented on ornately-styled bases and some were decorated with grass or turf-like designs. The majority of nineteenth century bases, however, appeared as smooth oval forms. For the most part, these were simply decorated, sometimes high-lighted with nothing more than a simple gold or black line.[3] Many based models incorporate a small round opening in the base that was designed to serve as a quill holder.

In some cases, bases were titled but this is not seen in Comforter Spaniel figures. Spaniels incorporated into titled groupings are sometimes seen and, of these samples (as well as in other figures of the time), titles were sometimes hand-painted in gold or black. Other titles were transfer printed in script, impressed, or presented in raised capitals. Gold script titles were produced after 1840, raised capitals printed in gold appeared until circa 1854 (black was used later), and transfer printing was used until the late 1880s.[4]

Grouped Spaniels

Spaniels often appear in family groupings of parents and puppies and in groupings of Spaniels with children and/or other human figures. In grouped Spaniel studies, as Clive Mason Pope points out, the Spaniels usually dominate the scene[5] and, although these figures are unquestionably delightful, they are most correctly considered satellite styles in relation to the traditional, seated Comforter Spaniel. Nearly all figure groupings that incorporate Spaniels are considered rare today.

An image of faithful guardianship, "Dog Tray" is a well-known and popular figure titled after Thomas Campbell's poem "The Harper" (1836) and a song by Steven Foster. The example shown here has been presented in white, although multi-colored variations have been recorded. The title appears in raised capitals (unpainted in this sample) on a white oval base. This figure of a Spaniel and sleeping child tends to be pricey, especially when the color palette is comprehensive. 9". Circa 1860. Value: $1000.00-$1500.00. *Courtesy of Anita L. Grashof, Gallerie Ani'tiques, Scotch Plains, NJ.*

Remarkable paired figures that incorporate spill vases, children, and begging Spaniels seated on colorful, cushioned benches. At first glance, the color palette may appear arbitrary but closer inspection reveals thoughtful planning. The interesting interpretation of natural hues in the spill vases introduces "ocherous" tones while the children, possibly members of the royal family, are brightly clad in green, red, orange, pink, and cobalt blue, all "primary" Staffordshire colors. The Spaniels, colored only in black and white, become, by contrast, the focal point of the composition. Careful organization in this grouping lends an almost photographic quality to the pottery which suggests that the children might be posing with their pets for a daguerreotype to be taken. 6.75". Circa 1850. Value: $1250.00-$1350.00. *Courtesy of Perry Joyce Antiques.*

Glass-Eyed Spaniels

The standard Comforter Spaniel is normally represented with hand-painted yellow eyes rimmed in black and sometimes detailed with black eyelashes and eyebrows. Nevertheless, a number of Comforter figures were made with glass inset eyes.

Although glass eyes became popular in children's dolls as early as the 1830s, most glass-eyed Spaniels date to no earlier than 1860 and, most often, later. Nearly all glass-eyed Spaniels were painted with Bright Gold, hence the dates assigned. It is probable that glass eyes were added to boost the market potential at some point when consumer interest had waned. Glass eyes may have re-sparked buyer attention, but their addition was less cost- and labor-efficient than painted eyes.[6]

Today's collectors may find it difficult to locate a pair of glass-eyed Spaniels with the original insets intact as the original glass eyes often loosened and fell out. A Spaniel with one eye in and one eye out is not uncommon.

Glass eyes first appeared in dolls as early as 1830 but were not used for Spaniels until after 1860. Most likely, glass-eyed Spaniels were introduced to boost the market potential toward the end of the nineteenth century when consumer interest had begun to decline. Along with glass eyes, these wide-bodied Spaniels are also distinguished by yellow-rimmed muzzles. 12.50". Circa 1885. Value: $895.00-$995.00. *Courtesy of Marla W. Chaikin, William Charles Antiques, Shrewsbury, NJ.*

Recumbent or Lying Spaniels

Several models of recumbent Spaniels were issued by the potters, particularly during the 1850s and 1860s. These Spaniels are commonly referred to as lying Spaniels and show a winsome, obedient expression which makes one imagine that their masters might have just issued the command, "Down!"

Like seated Comforters, lying Spaniels were usually produced in facing pairs and were presented with tails curled inward and one front paw appealingly turned outward. A few designs include children seated on lying Spaniels' backs.

Lying Spaniels are usually seen in sizes ranging from five to six inches in height and seven to eight inches in length. Larger figures are very rare. Most lying Spaniels were issued in the usual colors and wear the characteristic collar, padlock, and chain. Less plentifully produced, and not as popular in their day as the seated Comforters, lying Spaniels still make attractive and interesting additions to a collection.

This white and gilt single recumbent Spaniel illustrates standard lying Spaniel posture. Although this figure was manufactured after the turn of the century, its mold design, decorating detail, and character are correct. 5" (height), 8" (length). Circa Twentieth Century. Value: $35.00-$85.00. *Author's Collection.*

Flower Basket Spaniels

Several models of Spaniels holding baskets in their mouths were produced in relative quantity during the mid-nineteenth century. These figures are especially pleasing and highly collectible. They are not commonly seen and are thus considered rare and desirable by collectors.

Most flower basket Spaniels are found in the range of five to ten inches in height and in the usual body colors. Their baskets are yellow, white, or brightly colored and contain pink, blue, yellow, and green blossoms.

The best sources for flower basket Spaniels are better antique shows and dealers who specialize in Staffordshire dogs. This type of Spaniel *has* been reproduced, but the baskets are usually separately molded, and their recent vintage is easy to detect.

Flower basket Spaniels of different sizes but nearly identical mold design and painted decoration. Delightful and rare, flower basket Spaniels are especially popular among collectors. Singles are seen from time to time; pairs are more desirable; but matching flower basket Spaniels of different sizes are the most unique and the most difficult to find. 10" (left), 7.50" (right). Circa 1850-1855. Value: $895.00-$995.00 (left), $695.00-$795.00 (right). *Courtesy of Jane McClafferty, New Canaan, CT.*

Disraeli Spaniels

The Disraeli Spaniel, familiarly named for Benjamin Disraeli who served as Queen Victoria's prime minister, is extremely rare. This Spaniel's presentation is much like that of the traditional Comforter but its distinguishing feature is a neat row of carefully curled forelocks said to mimic the center forehead curl worn by Disraeli.[7] In most samples, the curls are present on both the front and back of the Spaniels' heads. It would appear, too, that the majority of Disraeli Spaniels were decorated in black and white.

Disraeli Spaniels are especially distinctive but they are also especially costly and are among the most difficult figures to find.

This rare Disraeli Spaniel features a neat row of very small black curls across its forehead. Like many Disraeli's, it was molded with one separate front leg and was decorated in black and white (red and white Disraeli Spaniels are even more rare than black and white). Carefully detailed eye and muzzle areas complete the well-groomed appearance of this "dandy" dog. 9". Circa 1850. Value: $750.00-$850.00. *Author's Collection.*

All Disraeli Spaniels are rare and valuable but this figure is particularly so because it was modeled in the round with two separately molded front legs. Characteristic forehead curls dominate the face on which eye and muzzle areas were painted in light pink with red details. 6.50". Circa 1850. Value: $795.00-$895.00. *Author's Collection.*

The curled forelocks on most Disraeli Spaniels were repeated on the backs of the figures; most often, other body decoration was not. In this figure, shown previously from the front, both curls and body decoration were continued on the back, making it a rarity among rarities. *Author's Collection.*

Jackfield Spaniels

Jackfield Ware was produced by applying a glossy black glaze over a red earthenware body. The process is believed to have originated in the Shropshire town of Jackfield, England, hence the name. Reference to pottery-making in the Shropshire Jackfield dates to 1560, suggesting that the industry in that area is one of long-standing. However, an estate called "Jackfield," located in Burslem, hints at a possible local reference in addition to the town of Jackfield in Shropshire.[8]

It has been remarked that Jackfield Spaniels became popular during the decade that followed Prince Albert's death in 1861 and may have been a reflection of the black attire that Queen Victoria wore from that time on. Victoria's profound and prolonged mourning undoubtedly affected her subjects and black pottery Spaniels probably seemed appropriate to consumers who were touched by their queen's personal grief.

Most of the Jackfield Spaniels produced were decorated only with gilt and many appeared with sgraffito detailing. Small Jackfields are uncommon and most of the Spaniels found today are over nine or ten inches in height.

A very rare and eerie trio of Jackfield Spaniels with white painted sgraffito eyes. Jackfield Spaniels were produced by applying a black glaze over red earthenware. Although Jackfield Spaniels are not common, they do appear on the market. Unusual figures like these, however, are seen infrequently. Pair: 12"; circa 1870; value, $895.00-$995.00. Single (with one separately molded front leg): 9.50"; circa 1870; value, $550.00-$650.00. *Courtesy of Anita L. Grashof, Gallerie Ani'tiques, Scotch Plains, NJ.*

Spaniels with Spill Vases

An extremely rare find is a large Comforter Spaniel supporting a spill vase. Although many small figures incorporate spill vases (one commonly seen and widely reproduced is a small figure of two poodles, a quill holder, and a spill vase), large *Spaniels* with spill vases appear on the market irregularly and infrequently.

Poodle, spill vase, and quill holder combination. This model is extremely popular and has been widely reproduced. 5.50". Circa 1920. Value: $195.00-$295.00. *Courtesy of Anita L. Grashof, Gallerie Ani'tiques, Scotch Plains, NJ.*

Spill vases were, above all, functional but the Staffordshire potters drew upon an intimate acquaintance with the country farmhouse and devised decorative spill vases which, like the majority of their figures, were designed to rest against mantle walls.

During Victorian times, matches were expensive and were used only sparingly by persons of modest means. Long spills of rolled paper, which could be used again and again, were made to light candles, oil lamps, and pipes from a previously existing fire source (i.e., the fireplace). These spills were kept close to the hearth for handy access, and spill vases were designed to hold them. Because the interiors of spill vases were not glazed, they were never intended to serve as vases for fresh flowers (although there is some indication that they might, at times, have held dried arrangements).[9] The name "vase" is rather misleading.

Most spill vases feature either human or canine figures in simple but attractively composed groupings. The vase itself is generally tree trunk-shaped and colored in white, green, or green and brown with a bright orange inner area. Several dog-breed models, and a wide range of other figures, are presented with spill vases, but paired Comforter Spaniels with spill vases are rarely seen, especially in heights over ten inches.

This model is the only known seated Comforter and spill vase combination. It was produced in facing pairs and in various colors. Figures like the spill vase Spaniel illustrated here were potted during the late 1870s and 1880s and are almost always seen in the twelve to thirteen inch height range. 13". Circa 1870-1880. Value: $1000.00-$1200.00. *Author's Collection.*

Novelty Spaniels

Most everyone familiar with Staffordshire figures is aware that novelty figures of a singular and fanciful character were produced by the potteries. Various novelty Spaniels were potted in the form of jugs, tobacco jars, book ends, banks, and other *un*spaniel-like items. These Spaniels, along with other novelties, reflect an aspect of the tastes of their time and add dimension to already significant collections.

One novelty of particular note is the pipe-smoking Spaniel. Several models of Spaniels with pipes in their mouths were produced, most likely in response to Sir Edwin Landseer's famous painting "A Quiet Pipe" (circa 1829), an imaginative and amusing study of a dog smoking a pipe. By 1840, new etching and engraving techniques made it possible for famous paintings like Landseer's to be reproduced in widely-read periodicals, thus bringing the works of great painters and illustrators to the general public. New print-making techniques and the "rage" for art reproductions were concurrent with advances in pottery production, and the Staffordshire potters took full advantage of prints as inspiration for subject matter in their pottery models.[10]

While novelty Spaniels are not among the most frequently seen, they certainly occupy a niche all their own in the Staffordshire "kennel club."

This large Jackfield Spaniel is perhaps the most novel of novelties — Jackfield, begging, and pipe-smoking. Superior molded detail, regal black glazing, and effective gilt highlighting would be enough to distinguish this rare figure. Add the impressive size, the begging posture, *and* a gentlemanly pipe, and the figure becomes an exceptional treasure. (Because of the dark body color, the pipe is difficult to see; it extends just below the Spaniel's collar on the right-hand side of the illustration). 13.75". Circa 1870. Value: $1500.00-$1800.00. *Courtesy of Jane McClafferty, New Canaan, CT.*

Side view of the pipe-smoking Spaniel shown in the preceding illustration. *Courtesy of Jane McClafferty, New Canaan, CT.*

Beswick Spaniels

Early in the 1890s, James Wright Beswick opened a pottery firm in Longton, England where he specialized in the production of dinnerware and ornamental ceramics. Later in the firm's history, circa 1936, John Beswick, Ltd. began producing china animal statuary, including paired dog figures that resemble Staffordshire Spaniels. Most of these are white with gilt decoration and were potted as part of the Beswick Fireside Series. The Beswick Pottery became part of the Doulton group in 1973.[11]

Beswick figures form their own category of collecting and should not be confused with Victorian Staffordshire Comforters. Identification is easy as each Beswick figure bears the Beswick mark (and usually a number) on the underside of the base.

A Spaniel pair marked "Beswick England 1378-4." The right-hand Spaniel is both taller and bulkier-bodied than the left-hand Spaniel. Because this pair was produced by the slip-casting method, both figures are very light in weight. Although their posture, molding, and finishing details simulate the traditional Spaniel "look," experienced collectors will recognize their Beswick pedigree. 9" (left), 9.25" (right). Circa Twentieth Century. Value: $250.00-$275.00. *Author's Collection.*

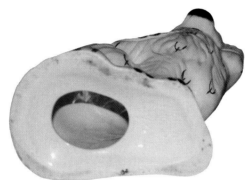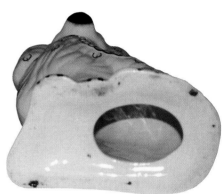

Bottom view of a Beswick pair showing the large holes left by slip-casting. *Author's Collection.*

A white Beswick Spaniel decorated with the characteristic gilt design. This figure, like all Beswick Spaniels, is identified as Beswick pottery on the bottom of the figure and is further identified by the model number "1378-3." 10.25". Circa Twentieth Century. Value: $185.00-$200.00. *Courtesy of Anita L. Grashof, Gallerie Ani'tiques, Scotch Plains, NJ.*

CHAPTER 6
• SPANIEL SIZES •

Sizes in General

Seated Comforter Spaniels were produced in a variety of sizes from about eighteen inches "tall" to two inches "short." Sizes varied from pottery to pottery but generally fall within these limits. The size of a figure is never as important as its condition, molding quality, color, decorative detail, and, of course, age. Collectors find it interesting to add figures of various sizes to their collections but the most eagerly sought, and difficult to find, reflect extreme ends of the spectrum, the very large and the very small.

While these Spaniels do not comprise a set (their bases are not numbered), they range from ten inches to three inches in height and illustrate the size variety available among figures produced in circa 1850. Versions of each of these were probably decorated in alternative colors as well as in the red and white shown here. *Courtesy of Jane McClafferty, New Canaan, CT.*

Sizes in Sets

The most common sizes of seated Spaniels usually range from twelve and three quarters to five and a half inches in height, with slight variations. A few potteries actually marked their model sizes by impressing numbers on the bottoms of the figures. It is possible, but certainly unusual, to see complete sets of Comforter Spaniel pairs marked from number one to number six with number one being the largest and number six the smallest. According to Clive Mason Pope, the set sizes range as follows:

Number	Size
Number One	12.75"
Number Two	10"
Number Three	9"
Number Four	7.75"
Number Five	6.50"
Number Six	5.50" [1]

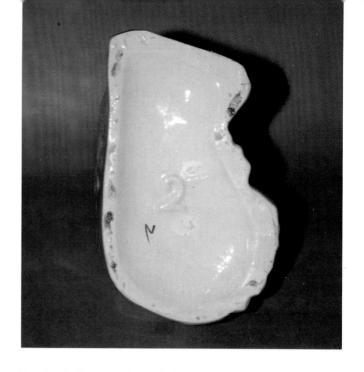

Despite the fact that the majority of potteries did not mark their Spaniels, figures are occasionally seen with numbered bases. When seen, numbers range from one to six, with one indicating the tallest Spaniel size. Most likely, numbers facilitated cataloging and ordering. The raised number two shown here was found on a 10 inch Spaniel produced during the early 1850s. *Author's Collection.*

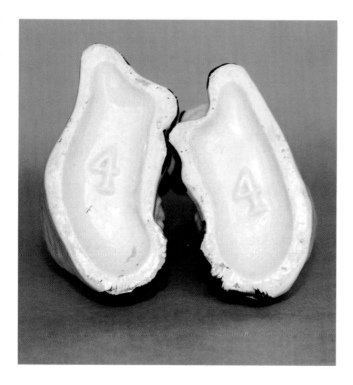

The number four as it appears on the bases of 7.75 inch paired Spaniels produced during the 1850s. *Courtesy of Perry Joyce Antiques.*

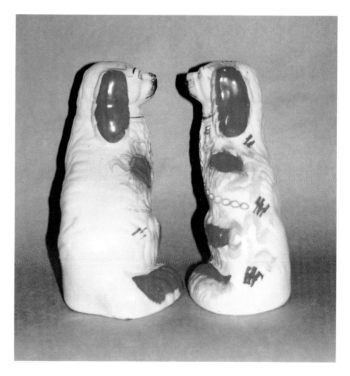

Although most Spaniel figures are characterized by a basic frontality, they vary widely in style and size. In this case, "widely" is no mere pun. The figures shown here are similar in size, mold design, painted detail, and time of manufacture (1850) but the Spaniel on the left is much wider in girth than the Spaniel on the right. Such variety was common within individual potting firms as well as from company to company. *Courtesy of Anita L. Grashof, GallerieAni'tiques, Scotch Plains, NJ.*

Form and Dimension

Although they appear in a range of heights, most seated Spaniel figures are characterized by a basic "frontality," in keeping with their flat-back chimney ornament function. Additional size variation among the flat-backs was achieved through body form and dimension. Many Spaniels are slim and elegant while others are bulky-bodied, broad-backed, or wide in girth. This kind of molding variety distinguishes similarly sized and decorated Spaniels from one another and it is not unusual to find Spaniels of comparable heights and colors with different body measurements.

Miniature Spaniels

Miniature Spaniels in heights of two to five inches were potted along with the more common sizes. Mini-Spaniels are extremely rare with more singles available than pairs. Tiny, and utterly enchanting, these "puppies" appear seated, incorporated into diminutive quill and ring holders, playing on cushions, and grouped with parents and other puppies. There is even an extraordinary and very rare Poodle-and-Spaniel-puppy combination. Some mini-Spaniels may have been made for children, like the children's dinner and tea sets produced in Staffordshire, and breakage and loss under the rigors of play would account for their scarcity today. Other small Spaniels may have been salesmen's samples, produced in miniature to facilitate easy carrying and to illustrate the styles and colors available to consumers who might wish to order Spaniels of similar design in larger sizes.

An extremely rare Poodle/Spaniel combination in which miniature white Poodles cradle even tinier red and white Spaniels between their front and back paws. 4". Circa 1850. Value: $795.00-$895.00. *Courtesy of Jane McClafferty, New Canaan, CT.*

The "Mr. and Mrs." Thesis

It has been noted that a Comforter pair often includes one Spaniel which is slightly larger than its companion piece. A commonly held theory suggests that Spaniel pairs were deliberately created to feature a female and a slightly larger male. Minimal height differences would be expected as no two left and right molds were exactly alike, but there is no documentation to prove that Spaniel pairs were modeled to create a "Mr. and Mrs." look. It is likely that the timing of mold changes within pairs did not always coincide; this would have resulted in slight size differences between paired figures. Another possibility is that with so many pairs being produced, some were mismatched at the factories. It is also eminently possible that, through the years, surviving single Spaniels have been matched with similar singles to form a "marriage"[2] which can be identified through close inspection of molding and finishing details.

Many collectors are adamant both for and against the "Mr. and Mrs." thesis, but neither side can prove its case. Relative information was either never recorded or has yet to surface. The fanciful idea of "mated" pairs *is* appealing though and perhaps a few of the original sculptors *did* indulge in a bit of romantic whimsy when they modeled their Spaniel pairs, Adam-and-Eve-style, from the rough material of clay.

These white and gilt Spaniels, purchased as a pair, have creamy white bodies and bright orange muzzles; however, their molding differences are quite pronounced and they are slightly different in height. The glaze on the left-sided figure is slightly rougher than the right-sided model's. It is likely that they were mismatched at the pottery or "married" at some time after their production. 7.75" (left), 7.50" (right). Circa 1870-1875. Value: $475.00-$575.00. *Author's Collection.*

CHAPTER 7
•FORGERIES, FAKES, AND REPRODUCTIONS•

An unfortunate fact of collecting is that whenever a particular item becomes popular, and therefore increases in price, reproductions begin to appear on the market. This is especially true of *antiques* and is no less true in the case of Staffordshire Spaniels (among the most widely reproduced Victorian-era collectibles).

There are three main categories of "buyer bewares" pertaining to Staffordshire figures. These are explained in detail by P. D. Gordon Pugh and are summarized here in reference to Comforter Spaniels:

1. Forgeries — copies of Staffordshire figures manufactured intentionally for the purpose of deception. The key word is "intentionally." Proving that a particular item is a forgery depends upon proving that it was created specifically for fraudulent purposes. In other words, forged Spaniels are those which have been created to *look* genuine, and are offered for sale as such.

2. Fakes — authentic Spaniels which have been altered or restored in such a way as to change the essential character of the figure for the dual purpose of deceiving the buyer and increasing the price.

Buyers beware! These large, dramatic Spaniels, each with two separately molded front legs, are very new reproductions. Although they look similar to the exemplary pair shown in Clive Mason Pope's book (see figure 42, page 97), they lack the spontaneous presence of genuine Spaniels. The first clues to these Spaniels' recent manufacture are large release holes and bottom areas that are not completely glazed. Closer scrutiny reveals problems with color palette, gilding, and a color-tinted glaze. Differences in painted detail simulate an authentic appearance, but detailing on the muzzles is too deliberate in this "too good to be true" pair. These Spaniels are listed in Staffordshire reproduction catalogs and may be among the new repros currently being made in China. 11". Circa 1990. Value: Under $75.00. *Author's Collection.*

3. Reproductions — copies made to be sold as copies. When honestly represented, reproductions lack the criminal intent behind forgeries. Sometimes reproductions are deliberately chipped or artificially crazed to lend an antique look. If these pieces are sold as reproductions, they present no problem. The biggest concern involves Spaniels produced and sold as reproductions but which fall into the hands of subsequent sellers who misrepresent the items as authentic. Many reproductions have been altered (they may, for example, be chipped and artificially crazed) and "passed off" to unsuspecting buyers as the "real thing." Newer factory marks have been removed as well for the same purpose. In such cases, these reproductions have moved to the category of forgeries.[1]

business. Numbers of Spaniels were produced from these molds during and just after the generally accepted period of production. To the purist, such Spaniels fall beyond the pale, although some are actually quite old and collectible in their own right.

Sampson Smith and John Lloyd were the only Victorian-era potters who used factory marks. In Sampson Smith's case, the pottery he founded continued to produce figures from the time of his death in 1878 until 1963. About sixty old press-molds, the majority of which were two-part Spaniel molds, were discovered in storage at the Sampson Smith factory in 1948. New figures and Spaniels were produced from the old molds and, while Spaniels marked with any of the Smith marks may generate initial excitement, they *are* found on reproductions and must be carefully assessed.[2] Newer marked Spaniels include those manufactured by William Kent (Porcelains), Ltd.

A trio of small white recumbent Spaniels produced during the twentieth century and virtually triplets. Several pairs of these Spaniels have been observed at recent shows and at flea markets, offered for as little as $45.00 to as much as $350.00 per pair. *Author's Collection.*

Because most Spaniels were unmarked, their reproductions can be created without the need of forged signatures or factory marks. The simplicity of their design also makes them an easy mark for enterprising forgers who keep an eye on the market.

Some reproductions have been made from original molds reissued by the pottery firms at later dates. Other molds were sold when potteries went out of

which produced Staffordshire reproductions until 1962, at which time some of the Kent molds were purchased by other companies.[3]

Significant numbers of new Staffordshire figures, many of which are Spaniels, are currently being manufactured in China. These figures have begun to appear in quantity in various international markets. Chinese-made Spaniels include pairs, recumbent Spaniels, parent and pup combinations, and Spaniel and children groupings. Most of the Chinese reproductions have small release holes and are closer in weight to authentic figures than slip-cast reproductions are. However, the rims of base areas are not completely glazed as they are in nineteenth century samples. Buyers should be aware that the Chinese figures appear with color-enhanced crazing and have been sprayed with a color-tinted glaze to create an age-worn look. Handpainted details are generally well done but include streaks and daubs of paint that look deliberate and harsh in comparison to the more unstudied painting on genuine figures. Unfortunately, thousands of these figures are currently being sold by catalog and mail order.

Discerning and practiced buyers know that the old clay, glazing, and coloring formulas are not easily reproduced, and visual distinctions between old and new figures are clear. Beginning collectors should always exercise a huge *caveat emptor* and be on the look-out for reproductions. Even if the molding "rings true" (particularly in the case of reproductions cast from old molds), the clay, glazing, color palette, and finishing details will lack a look of authenticity. Beyond any doubt, reproductions never possess the unconscious charm, the inherent dignity, and the spontaneous appeal of the genuine article.

Sampson Smith mark dated 1851. This mark was *established* in 1851 but was used long after that date. It appears on many figures that were produced until circa 1960 from original molds found in 1948. *Author's Collection.*

The William Kent Potteries remained in operation from 1844 until 1962. The Kent mark shown here, found on the bases of Staffordshire Spaniels and other dog-breed figures, includes the words "made in" before the country of origin which indicates a production date of 1920 or later. The inverted number "83" is probably a mold number, and the initial "M" probably refers to a particular pottery worker. *Courtesy of Anita L. Grashof, Gallerie Ani'tiques, Scotch Plains, NJ.*

CHAPTER 8

• TIPS FOR COLLECTORS •

Clearly, before one embarks on serious Spaniel collecting, it is a good idea to research the topic thoroughly. Beyond that, there is no replacement for hands-on experience. Museums offer an excellent venue for visual contact, but museums do not allow handling. While handling valuable and breakable items is, understandably, not encouraged in shops and at shows, sincere interest is usually recognized, and most dealers will be helpful in providing prospective buyers with reasonable hands-on contact. Visiting other collectors and sharing information and experience is always a good way to enhance one's own knowledge. Examining known reproductions as a basis for comparison is also an effective learning tool.

Following is a list arranged in two parts. The first part deals with general suggestions and *caveats* for prospective Spaniel buyers. The second part deals specifically with factory marks. "Grooming" tips for Spaniel care and cleaning follow the list.

General Suggestions

1. Buy only from established and reputable dealers whose good reputations have been earned though honest sales. This is especially helpful if one is a beginning collector.

2. Look very closely at the Spaniel under consideration. Examine its surface appearance to determine whether or not it has a patina, a mellowed look of age, or a "deliberate" old appearance.[1]

3. Measure the size of the holes on the bottom or back of a given Spaniel. These should be smaller than the diameter of a pencil. Anything larger is always suspect.[2]

4. Be suspicious of Spaniels made by the slip-casting method. *Some* were made during the nineteenth century, but *many* have appeared since 1900. Slip-cast Spaniels usually have open bottoms or large release holes (dime-sized or larger), and they are lighter in weight than press-molded Spaniels.[3]

5. Take special notice of colors, particularly white. Older Spaniels are a warm off-white rather than stark-white. Many have a creamy look. Reds should be muted, never crimson. Yellows, greens, and blues do not appear in body decoration, although yellow was often used for eyes and was occasionally used for collars, padlocks, and chains.

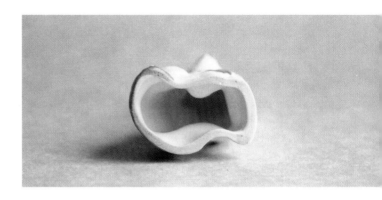

A completely open bottom always indicates slip-casting, a molding process used infrequently in Victorian-era Spaniel production but extensively in modern reproductions. *Courtesy of Jean A. Fromer, South Plainfield, NJ.*

6. Observe painted details. Genuine Spaniels usually show some measure of fine brush strokes while new Spaniels show evidence of having been painted with sponges or swabs (this is especially noticeable in the eye and muzzle areas). Many old Spaniels, while not always back-molded in great detail, generally show some painting on the back surface; most new Spaniels often have no painting whatever on the back.[4]

7. Check the weight of a Spaniel in question. If it feels unusually heavy for its size, closer inspection is warranted. Spaniels which have been repaired with plaster take on additional weight.[5]

8. Be wary of gold collars, padlocks, chains, and body decorations that are overly bright. Best gold, with its softer tones, was used primarily on older Spaniels. The gold used on more recent Spaniels is reflective and mirror-bright.[6] Best gold usually shows some signs of wear, but this does not seriously detract from the Spaniel's value.

9. Expect members of a Spaniel pair to be slightly different. Don't trust a Spaniel pair in which both figures are perfectly matched. Old Spaniel pairs rarely are but the differences should be subtle. Because genuine Spaniels were hand-painted, brush strokes and placement of designs were not identical in paired Spaniels. Today's sophisticated mass production techniques result in Spaniel pairs in which the figures are virtually twins.[7] Comparing facial features in a pair is a good place to start.

Painted decoration is usually applied to new paired Spaniels in an identical manner. An example of this may be seen in the reproduction pair shown here. Spots on the face, chest, back, and hind legs are the same on each of the dogs, as indicated by the arrows. Notice, too, the same placement of star-shaped designs on the front legs. The "look" is deliberate and unimaginative, completely lacking in the spontaneous appeal of genuine, hand-painted Spaniel pairs. *Illustration Courtesy of Antique & Collectors Reproduction News, Box 71174, Des Moines, IA 50325, (515) 270-8994.*

It is normal to expect differences in painted decoration on genuine paired Spaniels. The 1850s pair shown here illustrate differences in the size, placement, and number of hand-painted details. The Spaniel on the left has a larger series of painted marks at the top of the front leg than its companion does. In addition, the Spaniel on the right has a small group of stripes near the padlock that is missing on the left-sided Spaniel. Painted patches on the rear haunches of each are differently sized and the gold on the padlocks is unequally worn, as would be expected in older figures. The spots on these Spaniels are feathered and show greater attention to detail than is usually found in reproductions. *Illustration Courtesy of Antique & Collectors Reproduction News, Box 71174, Des Moines, IA 50325, (515) 270-8994.*

The gold used on Spaniel figures is often a good indicator of age. Most Spaniels have some gold decoration, usually in the collar, padlock, and chain area. Although such detail was sometimes painted in other colors on older figures (and on miniature figures in particular), the greatest number were gilded. Bright gold, introduced in 1860 and named for its bright, mirror-like quality, does not have the soft golden tone of best gold, which was used exclusively before 1860. In this illustration, the new gold on a reproduction Spaniel is highly reflective, in fact, the padlock actually mirrors printed material which was held about six inches away when the photo was taken. *Illustration Courtesy of Antique & Collectors Reproduction News, Box 71174, Des Moines, IA 50325, (515) 270-8994.*

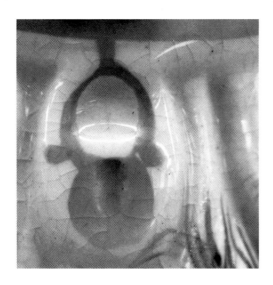

Gilding on all Spaniels produced before 1860, and on some figures produced after that date, is soft in appearance. It is never brassy or reflective, and generally shows signs of wear. *Illustration Courtesy of Antiques & Collectors Reproduction News, Box 71174, Des Moines, IA 50325, (515) 270-8994.*

10. Check crazing carefully and don't be fooled by it. Fine lines on the surface of any pottery product are not necessarily a benchmark of age. Many authentic Spaniels *are* crazed, but many are not. Crazing can be (and is) intentionally created in new pottery to simulate a look of age (sometimes black shoe polish is rubbed into the craze lines to heighten the effect). Crazing is never a reliable indicator of authenticity.[8]

11. Always insist on removing felt pads, especially if they are large, that may be placed on the bottom of a Spaniel. Often such pads are used to protect furniture surfaces but they are also used to cover the openings left by slip-casting.[9] It is a good idea to remove all materials (tape, price tags, notations of date) from a Spaniel figure. Reputable dealers will not mind being asked to do so and those who do mind might have something to hide.

12. Be careful of perfect, clean bases or bottom areas. The glaze on an old Spaniel is normally consistent over the entire figure. On many post-1900 Spaniels, areas that are not viewable are not completely glazed. The glaze on old Spaniels also shows equal signs of wear in terms of crazing or stressing.

These 12.75 inch red and white Spaniels are classic Comforters of the 1860s that have "seen better days." Unfortunately, poorly-done restorations, particularly on the left-sided figure, have committed the pair to the proverbial dog house and prove that restoration is best left to skilled and experienced professionals. *Courtesy of Anita L. Grashof, Gallerie Ani'tiques, Scotch Plains, NJ.*

Shown here is the right-sided Spaniel in the restored pair previously shown. A red enamel was painted over the original glaze in an attempt to hide imperfections but the color-match was inadequate at best and was applied so haphazardly that feathered details were lost. *Courtesy of Anita L. Grashof, Gallerie Ani'tiques, Scotch Plains, NJ.*

Additionally, old bases are often characterized by small pieces of debris, firing lines, ruptured bubbles, and paint drips.[10]

13. Keep in mind that a Spaniel pair is more valuable than a single Spaniel but pairs in superior condition are more difficult to find and can be much more costly. Be sure to examine both Spaniels in a pair very closely for any indication of a "marriage" (single Spaniels not paired at the factory but close enough in molding and finishing details to "make" a pair). Remember, too, that rare or especially attractive singles are eminently collectible and are a safe investment. Most importantly, rest assured that Spaniels purchased simply because they appeal to one strongly, for whatever reason, are often the "best" pieces in any collection!

14. Be alert to the fact that some Spaniels offered for sale may have restorations. A reputable dealer will point these out if he or she is aware of them. Use a fingernail to lightly examine the Spaniel's surface for changes in texture where fill-ins may exist, and check for discolored areas which might indicate older repairs. Ultra-violet light is the best way to determine whether or not restorations exist as repaired areas fluoresce under UV light. Acetone removes paint and glazing which makes restorations more visible, but it will also ruin a good repair.[11] Remember that, although restored Spaniels may suffer some decrease in value as compared to completely intact Spaniels, good restorations (especially those that are small and well-done) are far better than obvious chips and cracks.

The left-sided figure in the illustrated restored pair is a perfect example of high quality molding and painted detail ruined by breakage and subsequent disastrous restoration. Apparently, the Spaniel was badly broken and inexpertly restored with coats of plaster that have chipped and cracked. Surface areas that were painted over the glaze have flaked and peeled, giving the figure a mottled appearance. *Courtesy of Anita L. Grashof, Gallerie Ani'tiques, Scotch Plains, NJ.*

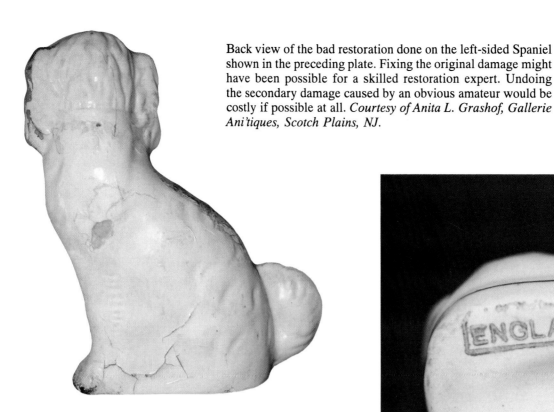

Back view of the bad restoration done on the left-sided Spaniel shown in the preceding plate. Fixing the original damage might have been possible for a skilled restoration expert. Undoing the secondary damage caused by an obvious amateur would be costly if possible at all. *Courtesy of Anita L. Grashof, Gallerie Ani'tiques, Scotch Plains, NJ.*

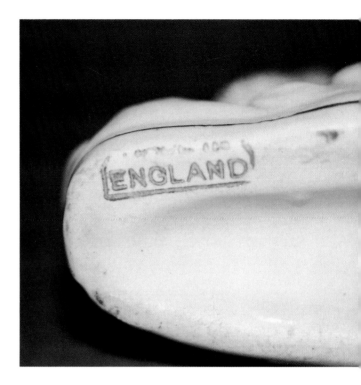

Post-1890 factory mark on the base of a late Victorian Spaniel. *Courtesy of Anita L. Grashof, Gallerie Ani'tiques, Scotch Plains, NJ.*

15. Make a practice of visiting dealers who specialize in Staffordshire figures. Study the Spaniels they offer for sale and ask questions. Don't feel uncomfortable about asking sellers to provide information on their Spaniels. Few Spaniels come with a provenance, but most dealers are only too happy to share whatever information they have regarding the background of a given piece. For insurance purposes, it is a good idea to ask the seller to note appropriate information on a receipt (size, color, approximate date of manufacture, and the price paid). If anything seems not right about a particular Spaniel, trust your instincts and don't buy it!

Factory Marks

16. Avoid most Spaniels with marked bases or bottom surfaces. Unmarked figures are the safest to buy *if* they pass all the tests previously set forth. If a figure is marked be very wary.

17. Stay away from typical recent marks that include phrases like "Old Staffordshire," "Genuine Staffordshire," "Staffordshire Pottery," and "Authentic Staffordshire."[12] Original nineteenth century Spaniels never bore such marks, and certainly none so ridiculous as "Old," "Genuine," or "Authentic."

18. Be aware that backstamps or transfers which include the word "England" usually indicate a production date after March 1, 1891 (when the McKinley

"New" Staffordshire mark paradoxically and revealingly uses the term "Old Staffordshire Ware." *Courtesy of Anita L. Grashof, Gallerie Ani'tiques, Scotch Plains, NJ.*

Tariff Act was passed and required that countries of origin be noted on products imported into the United States). Although the word "England" did appear on some earlier pottery products, old *Spaniels* bear no such mark while a number of later vintage do.

19. Avoid an anchor mark in gold applied *over* the glaze. This appears on some Staffordshire reproductions produced from circa 1930-1950. No mark of this kind was ever used on authentic Staffordshire pottery and, in fact, the anchor mark has been copied from a gold *under-glazed* anchor used on Chelsea porcelain.[13]

20. Notice worn or rough spots on the base or bottom surface of a Spaniel where a twentieth century mark may have been sanded or scraped off. A "Made in Germany" mark appeared in red ink on some circa 1920-1939 Staffordshire reproductions. This mark is reported to have been widely painted over or ground off on various figures.[14] Other marks proving recent manufacture have also been erased by dishonest sellers and the best and most easily recognized "give-away" is a spot on the base or bottom area that differs in texture from the rest of the surface.

Staffordshire bow knot used during the 1880s and found primarily on wares other than Comforter Spaniels. The bow knot is often incorporated into other marks used on later Spaniel figures. *Courtesy of Anita L. Grashof, Gallerie Ani'tiques, Scotch Plains, NJ.*

Gold anchor mark found on reproductions made between 1930 and 1950. This mark appears over the glaze; it is actually a copy of a gold underglazed anchor used on Chelsea porcelain. *Author's Collection.*

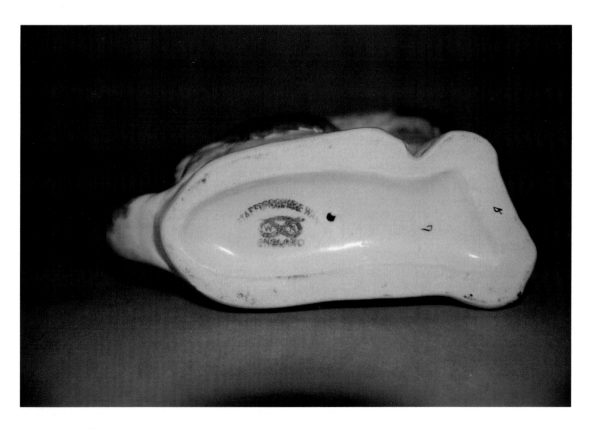

This Wiltshaw and Robinson factory mark has been found on a number of later vintage Spaniels. Inclusion of the country of origin indicates a production date of 1891 or later. (Wiltshaw and Robinson potted from 1890 until 1957.) *Courtesy of Anita L. Grashof, Gallerie Ani'tiques, Scotch Plains, NJ.*

Spaniel Care and "Grooming"

Like all pottery products, Staffordshire Spaniels need to be treated gently because breakage is always a concern. Exercising common sense in handling and display is a given. "Dog grooming," sometimes a must for Spaniel collectors, presents no serious difficulties. With a little TLC, even the grimiest Spaniel can be brought to a sparkling, "puppy parlor" appearance.

When necessary, Spaniel figures may be washed by hand in lukewarm water with a mild soap. Strong detergents, household cleaning sprays, and abrasive cleaners should be avoided, but dishwashing liquids and liquid hand soaps work well. A soft cloth or sponge is best for surface cleaning and a soft-bristled brush may be used to clean the face and other recessed molded areas where dust and dirt tend to collect. Soaking in water is not recommended as submersion may allow water to sccp into the body of the ware. Prolonged submersion will result in water entering the hollow interior through the escape holes. Extreme caution should be observed in cleaning enameled and lustered surfaces. These decorated areas are delicate and even the lightest rubbing may cause damage. After cleaning, air drying or drying with a soft cloth is suggested.

Occasionally, extra treatment is required for badly stained Spaniels and Spaniels with dark cracks or discolored crazing. Bleach should *never* be used. It is far too harsh and can damage the glaze. If a Spaniel is especially stained or discolored, it may be treated with peroxide, found to be the safest "bleaching" agent as it cleans well and will cause no glaze damage. Forty-volume peroxide is the most effective and may be purchased in beauty supply stores for less than $10.00 per gallon. The Spaniel should be placed in a non-metallic container large enough to hold the entire figure. The container should be filled with undiluted peroxide in such a way that the Spaniel is completely covered. It is best to place the Spaniel in the container in an upright position. A cover should be placed over the container. De-staining in peroxide usually takes some time and particularly stubborn stains may require several weeks. During the process, the Spaniel should be checked once or twice each week to determine how well the peroxide is working. Peroxide will lose its strength after a week or two and should be changed as necessary. The best way to test the peroxide's strength is to place one's hand into the liquid. If it causes a burning or prickly sensation on the skin, it is still working. If not, the container should be emptied and fresh peroxide added.

When the desired de-staining has been achieved, the Spaniel should be removed from the peroxide and washed in warm water. If any liquid has entered the interior through a release hole, place the release hole downward, allow the liquid to drain out, and then dry the figure's exterior with a soft cloth.

Some restorers suggest that the drying process may be completed by placing the figure in an oven set at 125 degrees. This low temperature will facilitate the process but will not damage the figure. To protect the glaze, both oven and Spaniel should be allowed to heat at the same time. In other words, do *not* pre-heat the oven. Fifteen to twenty minutes in the oven is usually sufficient. This step is a bit intimidating and may be eliminated, but be aware that, after weeks of "peroxide therapy," the figure will need a fair amount of time to dry thoroughly.

Spot-cleaning may be accomplished by soaking cotton balls or gauze pads in peroxide and applying them to stained areas. The cotton or gauze will need to be changed frequently.

Extensive repairs to chipped, cracked, or badly broken figures are best left to qualified professionals. Local museums and/or dealers who specialize in Staffordshire figures are usually able to recommend restoration experts with whom they have worked. Happily for collectors, skillful restorers can work wonders with even the most extensively damaged Spaniels.

CHAPTER 9

• *PHOTOGRAPHS AND VALUES* •

A selection of eight white Comforters which range in height from 14.75 to 7.50 inches. These figures give some idea of the different size and molding styles created by the Staffordshire mold sculptors from 1850 until 1890. Despite the obvious differences, these Spaniels are all characteristically similar. *Author's Collection.*

Photographs

The photographs included in this section represent a range of Staffordshire Spaniel samples and are broadly inclusive. Hundreds of thousands of Spaniels were potted during the height of their production and more than a representative sampling would result in a volume too unwieldy and far too expensive to be practical.

While examples of *most* Spaniel types are included, collectors are likely to find figures in their own collections that are very different as well as others that look similar but are not quite the same. It is interesting to note here that, despite differences in mold designs, sizes, and decorative details, the basic Spaniel form is very consistent. That fact notwithstanding, each Spaniel is unique because it changed hands several times during the potting and decorating processes and therefore carries each worker's personal touch.

It has been noted that models for one dog-breed often doubled for a number of others with minor feature changes. The same has been remarked about portrait figures. Molds representing certain royal personages were sometimes altered or retitled to portray other important persons and a local legend in Staffordshire holds that Obadiah Sheratt actually formed the udders on his cow figures from the same mold that he used for Wellington's nose. It would appear that the potteries had a "handle" on market-place tastes and were able to improvise and economize very effectively while keeping pace with an unprecedented demand for their wares.

Although the practice of changing titles did not apply to seated Spaniels, one *will* find strikingly similar features in various seated Spaniel figures. One reason for this is that older molds were sometimes altered and reissued at later dates while others were sold and used by their new owners "as is" or in slightly altered forms. Because Spaniels were largely unmarked, and because molds were often altered, reissued, and sold, dating presents a number of difficulties. With other Staffordshire products, backstamps provide clues to manufacturing dates (a potter's name may be traced to the time his pottery was in business and, thus, a date may be ascribed). This is not possible with Staffordshire Spaniels. For the most part, we do not know who the potters were and must rely exclusively upon stylistic features, molding and coloring details, painting and gilding styles, and the look and feel of any given piece.

One hesitates to mention that a few inconsistencies exist even among the most laudable studies of Staffordshire figures. These are explained by the difficulties inherent in the task. The potters themselves were not very cooperative, having left students of their craft little to work with in many areas of information gathering and sorting.

The photographs throughout this guide are accompanied by brief descriptions; figure sizes are noted; the earliest dates of manufacture (or approximations) are given; values are assigned; and acknowledgment is made to each person who made the illustrations available. Wherever possible, Spaniel pairs have been photographed but interesting and collectible singles are also well-represented. The figures in Chapter 10 have been presented chronologically from the earliest to the latest years of manufacture and a few photographs of commonly seen and/or unusual reproductions have been included for informational purposes.

Values

Values can be very difficult to specify because so many variables affect the market. The age and condition of an item are the most important factors to consider in price-fixing. In this guide, the value assigned is for a sample in mint or near-mint condition although the samples photographed may not always meet that criterion. Values will be appropriately higher for a matched pair than they are for a single Spaniel.

Spaniel prices vary from one geographic area to another. Correspondence with dealers indicates that values are not measurably lower in the mid-western United States than they are in large city areas in the east and west, although values in rural areas tend to be slightly lower than they are in big cities. Values in the southern Unites States are generally high. In England, where Spaniels are still sold in abundance, values tend to be up-market again in larger cities, and less costly in rural areas. The *general* rule of thumb seems to be big city, big price, but values sometimes have a lot to do with the dealer's buying price and the amount he or she needs to make on a sale. An interesting aside notes two New Jersey shops, located in adjacent suburban towns, in which almost identical copper lustered Spaniel pairs, in like condition, were offered at $675.00 and $895.00. Values at specialty shows and better auctions and sales are inclined toward the top end of the scale. Spaniels are sporadically offered at smaller auctions, estate sales, and even through ads in the trade papers. Pricing on these usually depends upon the sellers' expectations.

Given the factors affecting value assignments, it is impossible to offer price amounts that are "written in stone." The values suggested in this guide reflect current retail and auction prices and range from middle to high.

When it comes to values, the pure good luck of being in the right place at the right time is something every collector hopes for; and wouldn't it be wonderful if a time-traveling peddler carrying a tray of image toys were to knock on our door and offer us a selection of Spaniels for their original price of a few pennies apiece.

This single Spaniel, in mint condition, might realize a selling price of $600.00 or more but that represents the high end of the scale. A more realistic price would probably be in the range of $500.00-$550.00. However, if its paired figure were available, the two figures would be valued at $1200.00-$1400.00. *Courtesy of Perry Joyce Antiques.*

A Staffordshire traveling peddler carrying a tray of image toys. *Author's Collection.*

CHAPTER 10

• PHOTO ESSAY •
Spaniel Pairs

These first-class red and white Spaniels represent high quality in mold design and painted decoration. Fine feathering and intricately detailed eye and muzzle areas are skillfully rendered distinctions that create as aspect of energy and canine charisma. 10.25". Circa 1845-1850. Value: $895.00-$1025.00. *Courtesy of Anita L. Grashof, Gallerie Ani'tiques, Scotch Plains, NJ.*

This large seated Spaniel pair presents an engaging demeanor. All-white with best gold applied to collars, padlocks, and chains. 12.50". Circa 1850. Value: $895.00-$995.00. *Author's Collection.*

Fine details in both modeling and decorating lend a
Chesterfieldian stateliness to this large pair of red and white
Spaniels and distinguish them from other samples of their pro-
duction period. 12". Circa 1850. Value: $1250.00-$1500.00.
Courtesy of Jane McClafferty, New Canaan, CT.

Pair of red and white seated Spaniels with detailed molding
and painted decoration. The collars and padlocks on this pair
have been gilded with best gold and the chains have been painted
black. 10". Circa 1850. Value: $895.00-$995.00. *Courtesy of
Jane McClafferty, New Canaan, CT.*

Skillfully molded and handsomely decorated red and white
Spaniel pair. The number five is impressed on their bases. 6.50".
Circa 1850. Value: $695.00-$795.00. *Courtesy of Jane
McClafferty, New Canaan, CT.*

A striking pair of black and white Comforters. Distinguished
by strong molding and prominent painted detail, these Spaniels appear with a raised number two on each base, indicating
that they were the second tallest in a set of six sizes. 10". Circa
1850. Value: $895.00-$995.00. *Courtesy of Jane McClafferty,
New Canaan, CT.*

A small pair of exceptional black and white Spaniels which, like larger models of the same style, set the standard for excellence. A raised number four appears on the base of each figure, indicating that these were the third smallest in a set of six heights. 7.75". Circa 1850. Value: $850.00-$950.00. *Courtesy of Perry Joyce Antiques.*

A small black and white pair in which the right-sided figure has a subtly different tilt to its head, giving the impression that left-sided Spaniel is scowling while the right-sided is asking in surprise, "Who, me?" 6.25". Circa 1850. Value: $750.00-$850.00. *Courtesy of Perry Joyce Antiques.*

Small chunky-bodied black and white Spaniel pair with painted rather than gilded collars and padlocks. 7.50". Circa 1850. Value: $695.00-$795.00. *Author's Collection.*

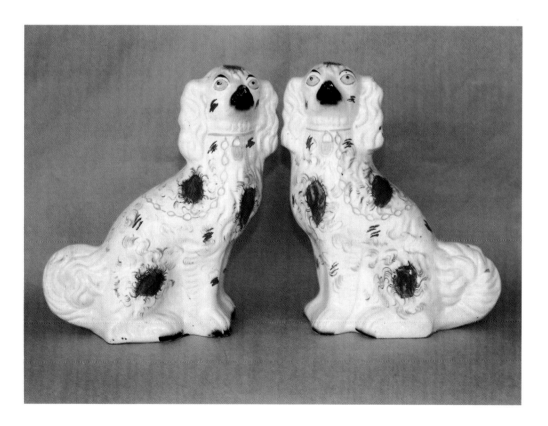

Unusual small feathered patches, wide yellow eyes, and yellow collars, padlocks, and chains give these tall Spaniels an individual and noteworthy character. Although it cannot be seen clearly in this illustration, the left-sided figure shows signs of having been burned, possibly when it was placed too close to an open fireplace — an "occupational hazard" for large Spaniels that were placed on the hearth. 13". Circa 1850-1860. Value: $895.00-$995.00. *Courtesy of Marla W. Chaikin, William Charles Antiques, Shrewsbury, NJ.*

Small, elaborately molded and decorated, chunky-bodied red and white Spaniel pair with a self-satisfied look. 6.50". Circa 1855. Value: $700.00-$800.00. *Courtesy of Perry Joyce Antiques.*

Lively red and white Spaniels sold as a pair but which differ slightly in size. Differences in molding and painted decoration, along with the size difference, suggest that these Spaniels may have been produced when a mold-change did not coincide, that they were mismatched at the pottery, or that they were "married" at some later date. 12" (left), 12.50" (right). Circa 1860. Value: $850.00-$950.00. *Author's Collection.*

Front view of a finely molded white Comforter pair. These
Spaniels are marked with the letter "V" on the center area of
both figures' front legs. 10.50". Circa 1865. Value: $895.00-
$995.00. *Author's Collection.*

Back view of the Spaniel pair in the preceding plate, showing
unusual molded detail on a flat-back. Although the molding is
finely rendered, no gilt or other painted decoration appears on
the backs of the figures. *Author's Collection.*

Painted black "V" that was painted under the glaze between the forepaws of the Spaniels shown in the preceding plates. *Author's Collection.*

An uncommon pair of black and white Spaniels with muted (almost blurry) eye and muzzle areas, unusual white noses, and red dotted nostrils. 9.75". Circa 1865. Value: $725.00-$825.00. *Courtesy of Jean A. Fromer, South Plainfield, NJ.*

Pair of white seated Comforters with unusual molding. The center part at the crown and the separately molded front legs are distinguishing features which give this pair a special character. 9". Circa 1865. Value: $795.00-$895.00. *Author's Collection.*

These paired black and white Spaniels feature separately molded front legs and black chains. 9". Circa 1865. Value: $850.00-$950.00. *Courtesy of Marla W. Chaikin, William Charles Antiques, Shrewsbury, NJ.*

Beautifully molded, and gilded with bright gold, these small white Spaniels are an attractive pair of confusing date. Use of bright gold indicates a production date of 1860 or later. The base holes are very small and the bottoms, which are unmarked and have been completely glazed, show the signs of wear associated with authentic figures. In general, the color and glaze appear to be old. Painted decoration is not identical on both figures, as it often is in reproductions. However, a number of very similar newer figures, with and without recent vintage backstamps, have been observed and indicate that the model *has* been reproduced. In this case, the conclusion reached is that these are probably genuine nineteenth century Spaniels or possibly very early reproductions. 7.50". Circa 1865-1875? Value: $595.00-$695.00. *Author's Collection.*

Pair of white Spaniels with purple collars, padlocks, and chains. A pottery worker's haste may be observed in the right-sided figure's collar and padlock which were not painted. 10". Circa 1875. Value: $695.00-$795.00. *Courtesy of Anita L. Grashof, Gallerie Ani'tiques, Scotch Plains, NJ.*

The red and white Spaniels shown here have the number two impressed on their bases. Apparently, at least two potteries numbered their models; the more finely molded and decorated figures appear with raised numbers and less detailed figures like these bear impressed numbers. 8". Circa 1880. Value: $695.00-$795.00. *Courtesy of Marla W. Chaikin, William Charles Antiques, Shrewsbury, NJ.*

The black and white decoration on the body patches and muzzle areas of these Spaniels was applied by sponge, a technique used more frequently on modern reproductions than during the nineteenth century. Molding and glazing qualities, carefully delineated eye and muzzle areas, and subtle differences in painted detail placement verify the authenticity of this rare sponge-painted pair. 10". Circa 1880. Value: $850.00-$950.00. *Courtesy of Anita L. Grashof, Gallerie Ani'tiques, Scotch Plains, NJ.*

Pair of primitive, sparsely gilded, all-white Spaniels. The lack of molding detail and painted decoration suggest a late nineteenth century production date. 10". Circa 1880-1890. Value: $595.00-$695.00. *Author's Collection.*

A primitive style and red "turned-down" mouths are common features of late nineteenth century Spaniels. Despite a difference in height and a bit more molding detail, these Spaniels were probably made by the same pottery, from the same mold design, as the pair shown in the preceding illustration. 10.50". Circa 1880-1890. Value: $595.00-$695.00. *Courtesy of Anita L. Grashof, Gallerie Ani'tiques, Scotch Plains, NJ.*

About the size of real King Charles Spaniels, these red and white Comforters would have been too massive to serve as mantle ornaments; most likely, they would have been placed at opposite ends of a hearth. 15.50". Circa 1890. Value: $995.00-$1025.00. *Courtesy of Anita L. Grashof, Gallerie Ani'tiques, Scotch Plains, NJ.*

White and gilt over-sized Comforters with nicely detailed molding. 14.75". Circa 1890. Value: $895.00-$995.00. *Author's Collection.*

These white Spaniels were gilded with small rosettes, some of which have worn away. The right-sided figure is slightly taller and bulkier-bodied than its left-sided partner. The distinguishing feature of this pair is their large, gray-painted paws. 9.25". Circa 1890. Value: $595.00-$695.00. *Courtesy of Anita L. Grashof, Gallerie Ani'tiques, Scotch Plains, NJ.*

Appealingly petite, these white and gilt puppies are just a bit too large to be cataloged among the mini-Spaniels. 5.50". Circa 1890. Value: $450.00-$550.00. *Courtesy of Anita L. Grashof, Gallerie Ani'tiques, Scotch Plains, NJ.*

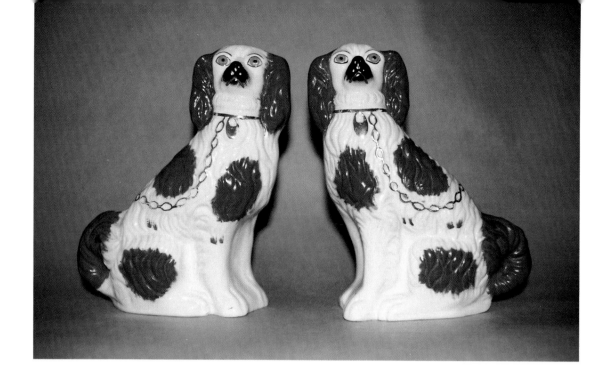

A pair of red and white Spaniels marked with the Wiltshaw and Robinson initials incorporated into a Staffordshire bow knot. The words "Staffordshire Ware" appear above the bow knot and "England" appears beneath. 7.50". Circa 1900-1920. Value: $425.00-$525.00. *Courtesy of Anita L. Grashof, Gallerie Ani'tiques, Scotch Plains, NJ.*

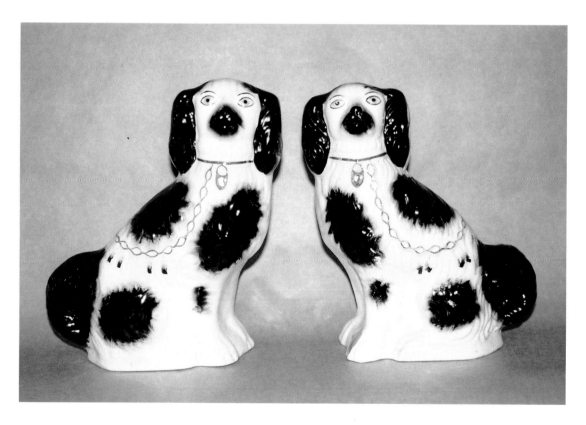

Black and white Spaniel pair of twentieth century vintage. Note the nearly identical size and placement of painted decoration. 9.75." Circa Mid-Twentieth Century. Value: $350.00-$450.00. *Courtesy of Anita L. Grashof, Gallerie Ani'tiques, Scotch Plains, NJ.*

Single Spaniels

An especially outstanding, early red and white single Spaniel with the finest feathered decoration, one separately molded front leg, and a bright spot of color on one cheek. Superb craftsmanship creates an aristocratic mien for this figure and sets a standard for quality that speaks of rarity and collectibility. 11". Circa 1845. Value: $795.00-$895.00. *Courtesy of Zane Moss Antiques, New York, NY.*

This unusual, early black and white Spaniel is distinguished by a separately molded front leg and very large front paws. Black overglaze enamel was used for all body decoration. 11.50". Circa 1845. Value: $625.00-$725.00. *Author's Collection.*

An attractive red and white single Spaniel, noteworthy for its fine molding and painted decoration. 7.75". Circa 1850. Value: $425.00-$525.00. *Courtesy of Nancy H. Furey.*

This thoughtfully molded and decorated red and white Spaniel features one separately molded leg and a large heart-shaped patch of red on its chest — the perfect Spaniel Valentine! 6.50". Circa 1850. Value: $450.00-$550.00. *Courtesy of Perry Joyce Antiques.*

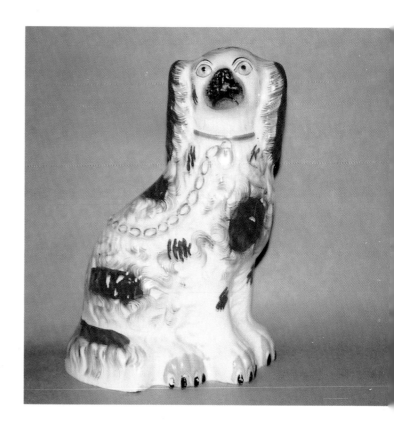

Red and white single Spaniel with fine, feathered body decoration and gray paws detailed in black. 10". Circa 1850. Value: $450.00-$550.00. *Courtesy of Nancy H. Furey.*

Wide-eyed and alert, this red and white single wears two round and two elongated patches of color that are finely and lightly feathered. The painted decoration on this figure is less bold than is usually seen in other samples of its style and production period and creates an almost pastel delicacy that is quite appealing. 10.50". Circa 1850. Value: $450.00-$550.00. *Courtesy of Anita L. Grashof, Gallerie Ani'tiques, Scotch Plains, NJ.*

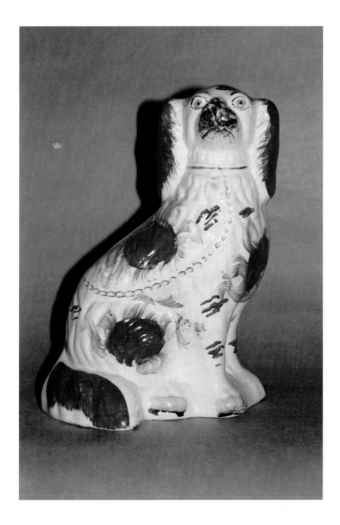

This red and white single Spaniel is similar to many of its production period. The figure has been decorated with special care in the eye areas as evidenced by carefully dotted lower eyelashes. The matte black of the enameled muzzle is sharpened by a red mouth. 10". Circa 1850. Value: $450.00-$550.00. *Courtesy of Anita L. Grashof, Gallerie Ani'tiques, Scotch Plains, NJ.*

A wide-eyed red and white single Spaniel wearing a bright spot of "rouge" on each cheek. 7.75". Circa 1850. Value: $400.00-$495.00. *Courtesy of Jean A. Fromer, South Plainfield, NJ.*

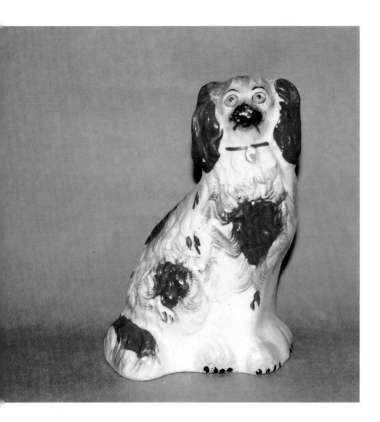

Small red and white single Spaniel with feathered decoration, gray-painted paws, and a gilt collar and padlock. As is the case with many smaller Spaniels, the chain has been omitted. 6.25". Circa 1850. Value: $375.00-$475.00. *Courtesy of Nancy H. Furey.*

This black and white Spaniel illustrates an uncommon variation on a familiar decorating theme. A white muzzle and vivid red smile give the figure a bold, noteworthy character and set it apart from models with similar lower body decoration. 10". Circa 1850. Value: $495.00-$595.00. *Courtesy of Perry Joyce Antiques.*

Fine molding and meticulous attention to facial detail contribute to an appearance of well-bred gentility in this black and white single Spaniel. 10.25". Circa 1850. Value: $450.00-$550.00. *Courtesy of Joan Gibbs.*

A "classic" single white Spaniel, nicely molded and decorated with best gold. 13". Circa 1850. Value: $400.00-$500.00. *Author's Collection.*

This lavishly feathered red and white single Spaniel is unusual in that its white chain makes an interesting contrast against the red painted decoration. Its paws are unpainted but are highlighted in gilt. 10". Circa 1855-1860. Value: $400.00-$500.00. *Courtesy of Jean A. Fromer, South Plainfield, NJ.*

A very rare white and gilt single Spaniel with one separately molded front leg and blue eyes. All blue-eyed Spaniels are rare; large blue-eyed Comforter Spaniels are almost never seen. 9.50". Circa 1855-1860. Value: $575.00-$675.00. *Author's Collection.*

A red and white single Spaniel with feathered body decoration and wide yellow eyes with dotted lower lashes. 13.50". Circa 1860. Value: $400.00-$500.00. *Author's Collection.*

This white and gilt single Spaniel is presented with a bright orange muzzle, finely detailed facial features, and black painted paws. 9". Circa 1865. Value: $325.00-$425.00. *Courtesy of Anita L. Grashof, Gallerie Ani'tiques, Scotch Plains, NJ.*

This broad-backed white and gilt single Spaniel is characterized by a proportionately small face, especially wide ears, and a neatly rounded tail. 12.50". Circa 1870-1880. Value: $425.00-$525.00. *Author's Collection.*

A slim, graceful white single Spaniel with sparingly applied gilt decoration. The detailed facial features contribute to a look of dignity and refinement. 9.50". Circa 1875. Value: $325.00-$425.00. *Courtesy of Anita L. Grashof, Gallerie Ani'tiques, Scotch Plains, NJ.*

A realistic fringe of fur on each ear is the unique and distinguishing feature of this brown and white single Spaniel. Although the potter and decorator were economical with molding and painted detail, this Spaniel's appearance is a significant departure from the norm. 10". Circa 1880. Value: $375.00-$475.00. *Courtesy of Anita L. Grashof, Gallerie Ani'tiques, Scotch Plains, NJ.*

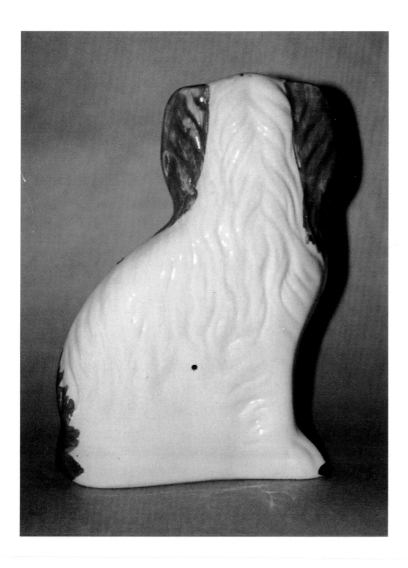

Back view of the Spaniel shown in the preceding plate. Note the interesting way in which the fur is parted at the head. *Courtesy of Anita L. Grashof, Gallerie Ani'tiques, Scotch Plains, NJ.*

This plainly molded and decorated white single Spaniel has the number four impressed on its base. 8". Circa 1880. Value: $325.00-$400.00. *Author's Collection.*

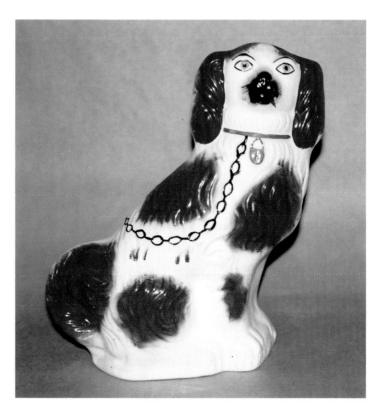

Similar to many Spaniel figures produced during the late nineteenth century, this single red and white seated Comforter lacks molding definition and fine painted detail but maintains its own measure of Spaniel "presence." 10.50". Circa 1880-1890. Value: $350.00-$425.00. *Courtesy of Anita L. Grashof, Gallerie Ani'tiques, Scotch Plains, NJ.*

An attractive, and rare, white and gilt Spaniel with unusual ears similar to those found in a small toy breed known today as the Papillon (French for butterfly). In this case, a "butterfly" character has been achieved with charming and fanciful effect. 12". Circa 1890. Value: $450.00-$500.00. *Courtesy of Anita L. Grashof, Gallerie Ani'tiques, Scotch Plains, NJ.*

Close-up of the molded ears which resemble the open wings of a butterfly, found on the Spaniel shown in the preceding illustration. *Courtesy of Anita L. Grashof, GallerieAni'tiques, Scotch Plains, NJ.*

A large, white single Spaniel, purchased in Ireland, which is both eye-catching and collectible because of its impressive size. 15.50". Circa 1890. Value: $400.00-$500.00. *Courtesy of Anita L. Grashof, Gallerie Ani'tiques, Scotch Plains, NJ.*

Large white single Spaniel with tail curling upward. Sparsely decorated with bright gold. 13". Circa 1890. Value: $350.00-$450.00. *Courtesy of Anita L. Grashof, Gallerie Ani'tiques, Scotch Plains, NJ.*

This tall, wide-bodied single Spaniel is highlighted in bright gold. 13.50". Circa 1890. Value: $375.00-$475.00. *Courtesy of Anita L. Grashof, Gallerie Ani'tiques, Scotch Plains, NJ.*

White single Spaniel with curled tail and pearly luster around the muzzle. 12.50". Circa 1890. Value: $350.00-$450.00. *Courtesy of Anita L. Grashof, Gallerie Ani'tiques, Scotch Plains, NJ.*

This red and white single Spaniel has one separately molded front leg and was slip-cast during the late nineteenth or early twentieth century. The collar, padlock, and chain were painted with a flat gold over the glaze. 9". Circa 1880-1920. Value: $375.00-$475.00. *Courtesy of Jean A. Fromer, South Plainfield, NJ.*

A white and bright gold Spaniel with two separately molded front legs. This Spaniel is an example of a style that became popular during the 1930s. 7.50". Circa 1930. Value: $225.00-$270.00. *Courtesy of Joan Gibbs.*

Lustered Spaniels

These copper lustered Spaniels with separately molded front legs are similar in style to others of their production period. A unique feature of this pair, however, is a soft purple "halo" seen around the collars, padlocks, and chains, caused by application of the copper luster. 10.50". Circa 1880. Value: $795.00-$895.00. *Courtesy of Jean A. Fromer, South Plainfield, NJ.*

Close-up of the light purple color around the collar, padlock, and chain on one of the Spaniels shown in the preceding plate. The metallic washes used in lustering were thinly applied and the underbody's color often affected the tones achieved by the luster. Copper luster, actually made from gold, turned purple or lavender on some white-bodied wares. *Courtesy of Jean A. Fromer, South Plainfield, NJ.*

A nicely molded pair of copper luster Spaniels, each with one separately molded front leg. 7". Circa 1880. Value: $795.00-$895.00. *Courtesy of David P. Willis, Plainfield, NJ.*

At nearly fifteen inches in height, this figure is the largest copper lustered Spaniel recorded. Not only is the figure singularly tall, it was also potted with a broad back and wide, barrel chest. One front leg was separately molded and the copper luster was carefully applied. The collar and padlock were lustered without inclusion of the customary chain (which, in this case, might have been "lustering the lily"). The size and imposing presence of this Spaniel make it rare, costly, and very collectible. 14.75". Circa 1880. Value: $1275.00-$1375.00. *Courtesy of Perry Joyce Antiques.*

This side view of the large copper luster Spaniel shown in the preceding plate illustrates how wide and massive the body of the figure is. *Courtesy of Perry Joyce Antiques.*

Expressive facial features, adequate molding, and bright patches of copper create a cheerful suggestion of vitality for this tall lustered Spaniel. 13". Circa 1880-1890. Value: $400.00-$500.00. *Author's Collection.*

Although the body molding on these copper lustered Comforters is not finely detailed, they appear with separately molded front legs. 9". Circa 1885. Value: $725.00-$825.00. *Courtesy of Anita Grashof, Gallerie Ani'tiques, Scotch Plains, NJ.*

Single copper lustered Spaniel with a separately molded front leg. Like similar lustered models, this Spaniel lacks molding definition and detail; it also appears with several spots on the face which were undoubtedly dripped by a pottery worker, a personal touch (albeit a probable indication of carelessness or haste) which adds to the Spaniel's uniqueness. 8.50". Circa 1885-1890. Value: $375.00-$475.00. *Author's Collection.*

Pair of reproduction copper lustered Spaniels. The lustering on these repros was not applied in the customary circular patches but, rather, in larger "splotches." The lustered areas are not identical, nor are the painted details on the muzzles. These decorative touches create a new but pleasant personality. 8.50". Circa Twentieth Century. Value: $295.00-$395.00. *Courtesy of Anita L. Grashof, Gallerie, Ani'tiques, Scotch Plains, NJ.*

This extremely rare single Spaniel is an example of the Jackfield Ware that was produced by applying a glossy black glaze over red earthenware. The development of the Jackfield process is generally credited to potters in Jackfield, a town in Shropshire, England. The technique was enthusiastically copied by Staffordshire, and other, potters. The figure shown here also features sgraffito eyes and one separately molded front leg. In addition, an elongated slot cut into the bottom and glazed suggests that this Spaniel was intended to serve as a bank. A one-penny coin bearing the likeness of Queen Victoria and dated 1901, the year of her death, was found inside the Spaniel. 9". Circa 1860-1870. Value: $795.00-$895.00. *Author's Collection.*

Back view of the Jackfield Spaniel shown in the preceding illustration. Areas where the black glaze did not completely cover
the red earthenware may be seen, especially near the bottom of
the figure. *Author's Collection.*

A one-penny coin dated 1901, with Victoria's image on the
reverse side, was found inside the Jackfield Spaniel previously
shown. The coin, possibly saved by the Spaniel's owner when
Queen Victoria died, had to be carefully extracted with a butter
knife through the coin slot in the bottom of the figure. *Author's
Collection.*

This extremely rare Jackfield Spaniel is distinguished by a separately molded front leg but it is even more remarkable for its unusual white-painted eyes which give it an almost otherworldly look. 9.50". Circa 1860-1870. Value: $500.00-$600.00. *Courtesy of Anita L. Grashof, Gallerie Ani'tiques, Scotch Plains, NJ.*

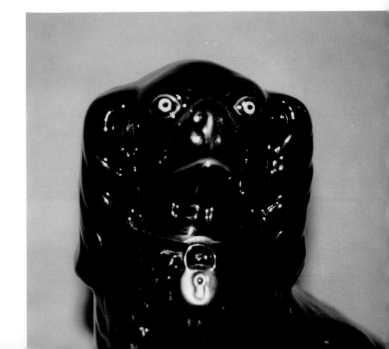

Detail of the white-painted eyes found on the Jackfield Spaniel shown in the preceding illustration. Note the realistic detail incorporated into the padlock. *Courtesy of Anita L. Grashof, Gallerie Ani'tiques, Scotch Plains, NJ.*

This elegant Jackfield Spaniel with gilt decoration is truly, tall, dark, and handsome. 13.75". Circa 1870. Value: $450.00-$550.00. *Author's Collection.*

Black single Spaniel of the Jackfield type. Highlighted in gold, this model has a regal presence that must have won favor among Victorian consumers. 12.50". Circa 1870. Value: $450.00-$550.00. *Author's Collection.*

A most unusual pair of Jackfield Spaniels with white-painted sgraffito eyes. The molding on this pair is well-defined and highlighted in best gold. 12". Circa 1870. Value: $895.00-$995.00. *Courtesy of Anita L. Grashof, Gallerie Ani'tiques, Scotch Plains, NJ.*

These tall Jackfield Spaniels are royally glazed and decorated with gilt. 13.75". Circa 1870. Value: $875.00-$975.00. *Courtesy of Jean A. Fromer, South Plainfield, NJ.*

A mid-sized Jackfield Spaniel with sgraffito carving, gilt decoration, and luminous glazing. 9.75". Circa 1870. Value: $425.00-$525.00. *Author's Collection.*

This unusual large Spaniel with closely cropped ears has been spray painted in apricot and white and sits on a low paneled base. Its inset glass eyes are amber-colored. 13.50". Circa 1880-1890. Value: $475.00-$575.00. *Courtesy of Jean A. Fromer, South Plainfield, NJ.*

Tall, chunky-bodied Jackfield Spaniel with inset glass eyes. 13.75". Circa 1880-1890. Value: $525.00-$600.00. *Courtesy of David P. Willis, Plainfield, NJ.*

Close-up of glass eyes in the Jackfield Spaniel shown in the preceding illustration. *Courtesy of David P. Willis, Plainfield, NJ.*

A pair of white and gilt glass-eyed Spaniels which were slip-cast and date to just before the turn of the century. Their bright gold decoration was applied in artistic circles and swirls, making these above-average figures particularly striking. 11.50". Circa 1890. Value: $795.00-$895.00. *Courtesy of June deBang, The Old Forge, Scotch Plains, NJ.*

Detail of glass eyes in one of the Spaniels shown in the preceding illustration. *Courtesy of June deBang, The Old Forge, Scotch Plains, NJ.*

Although much of its gilt decoration has worn away, this white glass-eyed Spaniel was once dressed from head to toe in golden feathers and swirls. 12". Circa 1890. Value: $525.00-$575.00. *Courtesy of Marla W. Chaikin, William Charles Antiques, Shrewsbury, NJ.*

Close-up of the glass eyes and muzzle decoration worn by the Spaniel shown in the preceding illustration. *Courtesy of Marla W. Chaikin, William Charles Antiques, Shrewsbury, NJ.*

Unusual apricot sprayed Spaniel pair with amber-colored glass eyes. These Spaniels were slip-cast and are surprisingly light in weight. 11". Circa 1900-1920. Value: $625.00-$725.00. *Courtesy of Jean A. Fromer, South Plainfield, NJ.*

Detail of the inset glass eyes in the Spaniels shown in the preceding illustration. *Courtesy of Jean A. Fromer, South Plainfield, NJ.*

Unusual Comforter-style dogs with inset amber-colored glass eyes. The mold sculptor might have had Collies rather than Spaniels in mind when he sculpted this pair, or perhaps he exercised artist's license and created an imaginative breed of his own. In any case, these spray-painted figures are obviously not old but their size and atypical appearance make them noteworthy. 13". Circa Twentieth Century. Value: $695.00-$795.00. *Courtesy of Anita L. Grashof, Gallerie Ani'tiques, Scotch Plains, NJ.*

Flower Basket Spaniels

A dainty and enchanting red and white flower basket Spaniel holding a color-coordinated basket of flowers in its mouth. 4.50". Circa 1845. Value: $550.00-$600.00. *Courtesy of Jane McClafferty, New Canaan, CT.*

All flower basket Spaniels are considered rare. The Spaniels shown here are especially so because flower basket Spaniels seldom appear on bases or in a standing position. These early paired figures are primitively painted in red and white with simple strokes of green on each base. 5". Circa 1845-1850. Value: $950.00-$995.00. *Courtesy of Zane Moss Antiques, New York, NY.*

An unusual pair of black and white flower basket Spaniels carrying orange baskets. Touches of gray paint were used to highlight the feathered patches and add to the visual appeal of this special pair. 8". Circa 1850. Value: $1800.00-$2000.00. *Courtesy of Marla W. Chaikin, William Charles Antiques, Shrewsbury, NJ.*

These black and white flower basket Spaniels carry yellow baskets filled with multi-colored blossoms. 7.75". Circa 1850. Value: $1850.00-$1950.00. *Courtesy of Jane McClafferty, New Canaan, CT.*

This red and white flower basket Spaniel is especially charming as well as extraordinarily well-molded and decorated. Like most flower basket Spaniels, its charm is enhanced by the guileless poise of the figure and the endearing counterbalance of the gift it appears to be offering. 6.50". Circa 1850. Value: $850.00-$950.00. *Courtesy of Jane McClafferty, New Canaan, CT.*

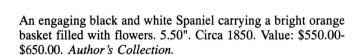

An engaging black and white Spaniel carrying a bright orange basket filled with flowers. 5.50". Circa 1850. Value: $550.00-$650.00. *Author's Collection.*

An artistically rendered white and gilt flower basket Spaniel, this model is large by category standards. Its distinctive coat style is similar in "cut" to that of the Staffordshire Poodles (without the use of slip to create a curly look), but is more specifically similar to the coat potted for the "Little Lion Dog." The main molding difference is the tail, which in Lion Dog models was thin, curved, and tufted at the end. A very rare flower basket Lion Dog, similar to this model and dating to 1850, has been recorded by Clive Mason Pope (see figure 2, page 117), and it is possible that the Lion Dog model served as inspiration for the unique Spaniel model pictured here. 10". Circa 1850-1855. Value: $895.00-$995.00. *Courtesy of Jane McClafferty, New Canaan, CT.*

A miniature red and white flower basket Spaniel with color-coordinated basket and chain. 4.50". Circa 1860. Value: $395.00-$495.00. *Courtesy of Perry Joyce Antiques.*

Still small at under 10 inches, this red and white flower basket Spaniel is among the larger of the flower basket models. 8". Circa 1855. Value: $895.00-$995.00. *Courtesy of Jane McClafferty, New Canaan, CT.*

This red and white flower basket Spaniel carries a bright green basket, a clever contrast that enhances the figure's wide yellow eyes and calls attention to the important upper portion of the figure. 7". Circa 1860. Value: $750.00-$795.00. *Courtesy of Perry Joyce Antiques.*

Recumbent Spaniels

This miniature black and white Spaniel is an early example of the recumbent motif. Fine molding and painted decoration enhance a lovable expression. The oval white base, uncommon among recumbent Spaniel models, is highlighted by a gold line. Well-traveled, this particular figure was manufactured in Britain during the 1840s, was taken to India at some point in its history, was found in Bombay during the 1990s by an American dealer who purchased it and shipped it to Florida where it was sold to a dealer from New Jersey. 2.50". Circa 1845. Value: $425.00-$525.00. *Author's Collection.*

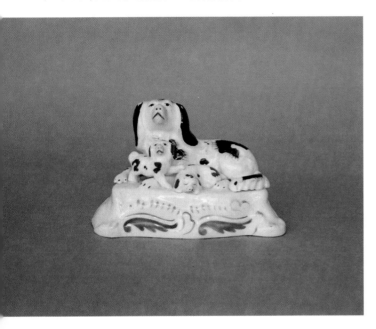

An exceptionally rare and fine figure grouping, modeled in the round, that includes a parent and two pups, one awake and playfully posed and the other napping. The parent is decorated in black and white, the pups in red and white. The elegant and elaborate white base is highlighted in gilt and includes two green acanthus leaves. Strong modeling and careful decorating make this a very unusual and collectible figure. 3.25". Circa 1845. Value: $795.00-$895.00. *Courtesy of Marla W. Chaikin, William Charles Antiques, Shrewsbury, NJ.*

A very rare, large white lying Spaniel with curled front paw and obedient facial expression. This authentic model has been widely reproduced, usually in smaller sizes. 7" (height), 10" (length). Circa 1850. Value: $1000.00-$1250.00. *Courtesy of Barbara and Melvin Alpren Antiques, West Orange, NJ.*

Princess Royal seated on the back of a recumbent Spaniel. Like most recumbent Spaniels, this figure was originally produced as one of a pair. 6.75" (height), 6.50" (length). Circa 1850. Value: $995.00-$1025.00. *Courtesy of Barbara and Melvin Alpren Antiques, West Orange, NJ.*

A pocket-sized pair of miniature lying Spaniels with children seated on their backs. The children in this tiny pair were decorated with brightly colored clothing but with primitive, indistinct facial features. The red and white Spaniels, however, received greater attention to painted decoration. Their body patches were nicely feathered and their facial features were rendered with greater clarity than those of the children. These figures are miniature versions of the lying Spaniel with seated child motif and, despite their Lilliputian size, might be cataloged as recumbent, miniature, based, or grouped with human figures. 2.75" (height), 2.25" (length). Circa 1855-1860. Value $795.00-$895.00. *Author's Collection.*

This miniature figure is almost identical to the left-sided figure shown in the previous illustration. Colored details, as in the boy's shirt and trousers, have been reversed, and the figure itself is exactly one inch larger. The figure shown here was originally potted as one of a pair. 3.75" (height), 3.25" (length). Circa 1855-1860. Value: $325.00-$425.00. *Courtesy of Anita L. Grashof, Gallerie Ani'tiques, Scotch Plains, NJ.*

These white recumbent Spaniels were manufactured in the typical style. Nineteenth century pairs are very difficult to find, and the Spaniels shown here are of twentieth century vintage. 5" (height), 8" (length). Circa 1920-1950. Value: $75.00-$175.00. *Author's Collection.*

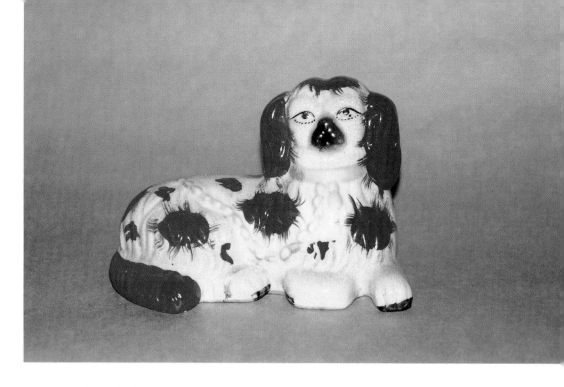

A slip-cast Spaniel of very recent vintage. Note the "lack-luster" expression of the eyes which makes this figure appear not-quite-right and less appealing than the earlier reproductions shown in the preceding illustration. 5" (height), 8" (length). Circa 1980-1990. Value: $25.00-$30.00. *Author's Collection.*

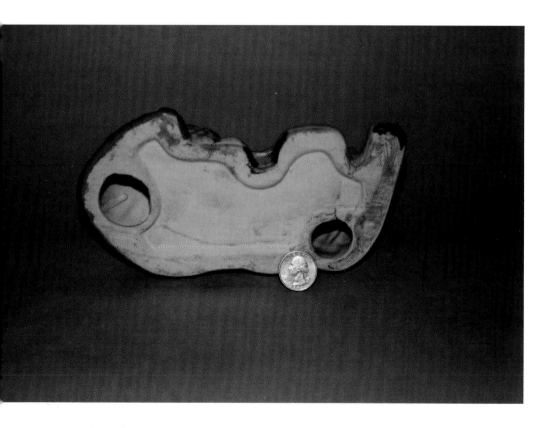

Bottom view of the slip-cast lying Spaniel shown in the preceding photo. A quarter has been placed next to one of the holes left by slip-casting to illustrate how large such holes usually are. *Author's Collection.*

These sophisticated red and white Spaniels illustrate a high level of excellence in molding and painted detail. The addition of curved lines to the separately molded legs adds a note of realism while artistically rendered facial features create an urbane, well-bred appearance. Unusually molded bases, highlighted in gilt, complete the elegant presentation. 7.75". Circa 1845. Value: $1895.00-$2200.00. *Courtesy of Jane McClafferty, New Canaan, CT.*

Miniature red and white parent and pup Spaniels on a white base which is highlighted by a thin gold line. The line's asymmetrical slant is evidence of a pottery worker's lack of skill, haste, or carelessness. 4". Circa 1845. Value: $375.00-$475.00. *Courtesy of Jane McClafferty, New Canaan, CT.*

This rare grouping includes a seated parent with a begging pup at her side. The Spaniels are colored in red and white and the oval base is decorated with a thin black line. 6". Circa 1845. Value: $595.00-$695.00. *Courtesy of Marla W. Chaikin, William Charles Antiques, Shrewsbury, NJ.*

A delightful pottery study of puppies playing. These tiny Spaniels were produced in the round and their raised quill holder bases were underglazed in cobalt blue with pink and green painted details. Ultra-miniature pairs on bases, like these, are extremely rare. 2.25" (height), 2.50" (length). Circa 1845. Value: $895.00-$995.00. *Courtesy of Barbara and Melvin Alpren Antiques, West Orange, NJ.*

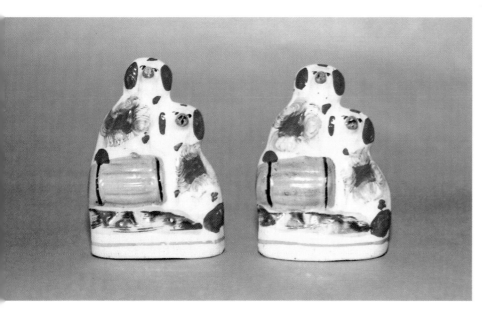

These primitive miniature barrel puppies are a less refined rendering of a motif that was repeated in sharper detail on larger, later figures. The pups in the figures shown here appear with little facial detail; however, some feathered brushing has been applied to the red body patches. The molding and decorating are undoubtedly simple but are charmingly effective. 4.50". Circa 1845-1850. Value: $695.00-$795.00. *Courtesy of Anita L. Grashof, Gallerie Ani'tiques, Scotch Plains, NJ.*

The model for these standing "Spaniels" with pheasants in their mouths is very similar to the based, standing flower basket Spaniels shown earlier. Although the dogs in both models are remotely like the Harrier breed, their long ears and curled tails are more Spaniel-like. It is unlikely that Spaniels would be cast as hunting dogs; however, because these figures were produced around the time that Spaniels were becoming popular, it is possible that the mold sculptor drew upon the once popular and the newly popular in designing this model. 5". Circa 1845-50. Value: $950.00-$995.00. *Courtesy of Marla W. Chaikin, William Charles Antiques, Shrewsbury, NJ.*

This attractive red and white Spaniel with one separately molded front leg is presented on a white oval base with a single gold line. Innocent and somewhat apologetic eyes suggest that this pup might be saying, "That spot on the carpet? Oops!" 7". Circa 1850. Value: $550.00-$600.00. *Courtesy of Perry Joyce Antiques.*

Miniature Spaniels colored in liver and white are always rare. These feature separately molded front legs and are seated on nicely molded white bases. Above average in quality, paired puppies like these may be small in size but are large in value. 3.50". Circa 1850. Value: $1250.00-$1350.00. *Courtesy of Marla W. Chaikin, William Charles Antiques, Shrewsbury, NJ.*

Paired miniature Spaniels, on cobalt bases, with two separately molded front legs. Interestingly, the gold line on the base has been placed at the bottom rather than in the middle as most commonly seen. 4.50". Circa 1850. Value; $1200.00-$1295.00. *Courtesy of Marla W. Chaikin, William Charles Antiques, Shrewsbury, NJ.*

These red and white mini-Spaniels share a white scalloped base. Two Spaniels on a single base are rare and whether or not this figure was potted as one of a pair is not known. 3.50". Circa 1850. Value: $475.00-$525.00. *Author's Collection.*

Red and white parent Spaniels modeled with pups at their sides. Bits of slip were added to create mossy seats for the pups. Skillfully molded and appealingly decorated, these paired figures are both delightful and rare. 5". Circa 1850. Value: $1250.00-$1350.00. *Courtesy of Marla W. Chaikin, William Charles Antiques, Shrewsbury, NJ.*

Seated on an orange cushion, complete with tassels and swag, are black and white parent and pup Spaniels. This rare figure is appealingly modeled in the round with effective contrast in painted decoration. 6". Circa 1850. Value: $795.00-$895.00. *Courtesy of Marla W. Chaikin, William Charles Antiques, Shrewsbury, NJ.*

While the mold design for the trio of parent and pup figures shown here is the same, no two figures make a correct pair. In each, strong molding is matched by thoughtful decoration and elaborate scrolled bases. Rare. 3". Circa 1850. Value: $550.00-$650.00 (one), $1100.00-$1300.00 (two), $2200.00-$2600.00 (three). *Courtesy of Marla W. Chaikin, William Charles Antiques, Shrewsbury, NJ.*

This outstanding little Spaniel has two separately molded front legs and is seated on a tri-colored, tasseled cushion. Attractive molding, a porcellaneous body, and an amiable expression add to the charm and value of the figure. 5". Circa 1850. Value: $495.00-$595.00. *Courtesy of Marla W. Chaikin, William Charles Antiques, Shrewsbury, NJ.*

This rare figure does not portray a King Charles Spaniel but, rather, an English Water Spaniel which is seated on a cobalt blue base. The once popular Water Spaniel is now an extinct breed in Britain. 6". Circa 1850. Value: $895.00-$995.00. *Courtesy of Jane McClafferty, New Canaan, CT.*

Shown here is another English Water Spaniel, elegantly posed on an unusual and elaborate blue, white, and gilt base. 6". Circa 1850. Value: $895.00- $995.00. *Courtesy of Marla W. Chaikin, William Charles Antiques, Shrewsbury, NJ.*

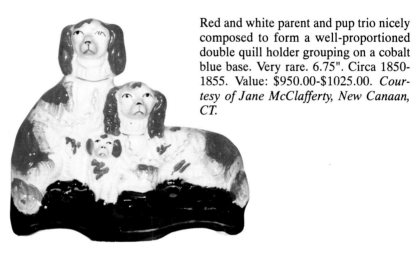

Red and white parent and pup trio nicely composed to form a well-proportioned double quill holder grouping on a cobalt blue base. Very rare. 6.75". Circa 1850-1855. Value: $950.00-$1025.00. *Courtesy of Jane McClafferty, New Canaan, CT.*

This double quill holder parent and pup model was shown in the preceding illustration with a cobalt blue base and more conscientious treatment of the eye and muzzle areas. Different workers, with different abilities and/or approaches to decoration, might account for the disparities in the samples shown. Another possibility is that this figure was produced from an older mold, at a later date, when less attention was paid to decorating detail. 6". Circa 1850-1855 (possibly later). Value: $900.00-$995.00. *Courtesy of Marla W. Chaikin, William Charles Antiques, Shrewsbury, NJ.*

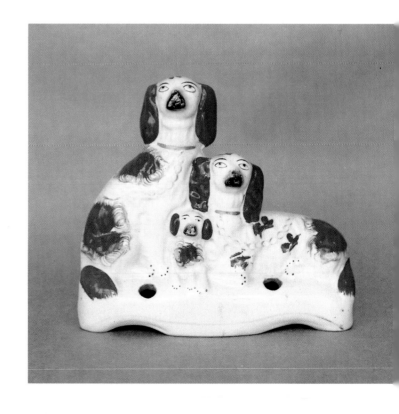

This centerpiece clock grouping includes a Poodle at the top and an alternatively colored Spaniel at each side. Variations may be seen with either three Poodles or three Spaniels. 9". Circa 1855. Value: $1200.00-$1300.00. *Courtesy of Marla W. Chaikin, William Charles Antiques, Shrewsbury, NJ.*

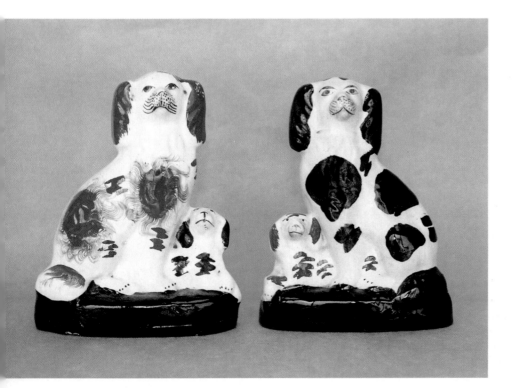

These parent and pup figures, decorated in alternate colors, were sold as a pair. Although the mold design is the same, the painted decoration is too different for the figures to have been correctly paired at the pottery. The most obvious differences, other than color, occur in the muzzle areas and in the feathering on the left-sided parent. Each figure is considered rare, and together these figures provide an excellent example of the variations achieved by the Staffordshire decorators when working with figures from the same mold design. 6". Circa 1855. Value: $650.00-$750.00 (each). *Courtesy of Marla W. Chaikin, William Charles Antiques, Shrewsbury, NJ.*

Extremely rare paired "wash basket" Spaniels set on oval, cobalt blue bases. Whimsically composed, these figures suggest a playful approach to wash-day chores. 5.75". Circa 1855-1860. Value: $2250.00-$2400.00. *Courtesy of Marla W. Chaikin, William Charles Antiques, Shrewsbury, NJ.*

These extremely rare figures show cupids, complete with bows, seated on the backs of red and white Spaniels. The subject matter is remarkable as are the graceful design, color palette, and cobalt bases cinctured with thin gold lines. It would appear that Cupid really did use his bow when it came to Britain's "romance" with King Charles Spaniels and the pottery figures they inspired. 6". Circa 1855-1860. Value: $2300.00-$2400.00. *Courtesy of Marla W. Chaikin, William Charles Antiques, Shrewsbury, NJ.*

This parent and pup grouping rests on a white oval base upon which traces of a gold line may be seen. The model for this figure was first produced in 1855, and figures of that date are usually seen with red and white parents and black and white pups. In this case, the decorator opted for white and gilt coloring. This, along with a lack of detail in the eye and muzzle areas, suggests a slightly later production time. 7". Circa 1860-1865. Value: $550.00-$650.00. *Courtesy of Marla W. Chaikin, William Charles Antiques, Shrewsbury, NJ.*

"Roll out the Barrel" would be an appropriate tune for this red and white Spaniel grouping. The figure is thoughtfully molded and finely detailed. Its subject matter is amusing and charming. But beware, this model has been reproduced in quantity. Copies currently appear in Staffordshire reproduction catalogs, and recent vintage figures have been seen at shows and in shops. 8.50". Circa 1860. Value: $695.00-$795.00. *Author's Collection.*

Roll out another barrel! This figure, while definitely authentic, is less finely molded and decorated than the figure shown in the preceding illustration. It is probable that both figures were produced by the same pottery. Either another, similar, mold was used or the same mold was well-worn by the time this figure was potted. While both figures are eminently collectible, their subtle differences present a convincing case for careful scrutiny of molding and painted details, both of which affect values. 8.50". Circa 1860. Value: $625.00-$725.00. *Courtesy of Anita L. Grashof, Gallerie Ani'tiques, Scotch Plains, NJ.*

An extremely rare example of a seated Spaniel supporting a spill vase. The white oval base is highlighted by a thin gold line. A newspaper spill dated January 5, 1883 (shown below the figure) was found inside the spill vase. 13". Circa 1870-1880. Value: $1000.00-$1200.00. *Author's Collection.*

Finding a large spill vase Spaniel is uncommon; finding a matched pair is nearly impossible. These red and white Comforters support green and brown spill vases with orange painted interiors and stand on white oval bases that were decorated to simulate grassy terrain. 13.75". Circa 1870-1880. Value: $2000.00-$2500.00. *Courtesy of Nancy H. Furey.*

These paired, red and white, spill vase Spaniels, like all others of the style, are presented on "grassy terrain" and white oval bases. The only differences among spill vase Spaniels of this type exist in the painted decoration and very slight differences in height. 13.50". Circa 1870-1880. Value: $2000.00-$2500.00. *Courtesy of Jane McClafferty, New Canaan, CT.*

Shown here is another variation of the decorating alternatives seen in the spill vase Spaniel model. The color palette for these models includes white and gilt and pale green, brown, and yellow which combine to create an effect of muted lightness in the otherwise heavy-looking figures. 12.50". Circa 1870-1880. Value: $2000.00-$2500.00. *Courtesy of Marla W. Chaikin, William Charles Antiques, Shrewsbury, NJ.*

Spaniels Grouped with Human Figures

This is a very rare figure of a young girl seated on a skirted orange cushion with a Spaniel beside her. The child's left leg is drawn up for the Spaniel to rest against and her right arm is companionably placed on the dog's head. 4". Circa 1845. Value: $625.00-$675.00. *Courtesy of Marla W. Chaikin, William Charles Antiques, Shrewsbury, NJ.*

A miniature pair of orange and yellow clad children seated on the backs of red and white Spaniels. A coordinated color palette includes yellow, rather than gold, lines on each base. 4". Circa 1845-1850. Value: $995.00-$1095.00. *Courtesy of Marla W. Chaikin, William Charles Antiques, Shrewsbury, NJ.*

One is tempted to entitle this figure "Guardian of a Midsummer Night's Dream." Like "Dog Tray" the subject matter focuses on a sleeping child and her dog. Attention to detail and painted decoration complement the mold sculptor's vision of childlike innocence and trust as the Spaniel-like dog guards his young mistress's dreams. 4" (height), 6" (length). Circa 1845-1850. Value: $450.00-$550.00. *Courtesy of Nancy H. Furey.*

Paired figures representing the royal children seated on the backs of dogs became popular during the late 1840s. Among the earlier figures, as seen in this illustration, the children were modeled on the backs of St. Bernard's. Interestingly, by the early 1850s, the children were shown more frequently on the backs of Spaniels. 9.50". Circa 1848. Value: $1800.00-$1900.00. *Courtesy of Jane McClafferty, New Canaan, CT.*

This single figure is identical to the right-hand model in the preceding photo except for the change in coloring. It was originally potted as one of a pair and illustrates the potters' versatility in creating different looks for figures produced from the same mold designs. 9.50". Circa 1848. Value: $900.00-$950.00. *Courtesy of Anita Grashof, Gallerie Ani'tiques, Scotch Plains, NJ.*

Poignant study of a sad child being comforted by a Spaniel. (Note the position of the Spaniel's paw.) This very rare figure is distinguished by sureness of design, realistic molding, and effective painted detail. 5". Circa 1850. Value: $550.00-$650.00. *Courtesy of Nancy H. Furey.*

Side view of the figure shown in the preceding illustration. *Courtesy of Nancy H. Furey.*

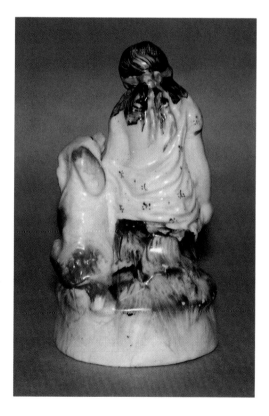

Back view of the sad child model. The formal composition of this figure is characterized by a simple harmony and suggests the mold sculptor's instinctive feeling for the natural beauty and decorative possibilities of his subject. An uncompromised color palette heightens the effect of realistic and graceful molding. *Courtesy of Nancy H. Furey.*

The ever-popular Spaniel/child grouping is simply expressed in this figure of a child seated side-saddle on a Spaniel's back. Modest painted decoration maximizes the effect of an uncluttered presentation and calls attention to the easy relationship between the child and the dog. 6.50". Circa 1850. Value: $650.00-$750.00. *Author's Collection.*

In this figure, a young girl sits properly side-saddle on a large red and white Spaniel's back while a parrot sits on her shoulder. Attention to detail in the upper portion of the figure is repeated in the elaborate, raised base that is decorated with grapes, leaves, and a gold line. Lavish detail notwithstanding, the Spaniel is the true focal point of the piece. 10". Circa 1850. Value: $1100.00-$1200.00. *Courtesy of Marla W. Chaikin, William Charles Antiques, Shrewsbury, NJ.*

A figure grouping consisting of a boy and girl, a white spill vase, a black and white Spaniel, and a tiny lamb (lying at the Spaniel's feet). A spray of flowers at the neck of the spill vase is complemented by the flowers held in the girl's skirt. Skillfully composed, this grouping is symmetrically pleasing to the eye. Its components suggest a pastoral springtime setting and a bright color palette adds to the "floral essence" of the piece. 7.50". Circa 1850. Value: $525.00-$625.00. *Courtesy of Glenbrook Antiques.*

The pointed snouts on these dogs suggest that they are Irish Setters rather than Spaniels posed with the Princess Royal and her brother. These figures illustrate the fact the other dog-breeds were potted in figure groupings but Spaniels were, by far, the most popular. 8.50". Circa 1850. Value: $1375.00- $1475.00. *Courtesy of Perry Joyce Antiques.*

Portrait figure group which incorporates a King Charles Spaniel. Represented here are the Princess Royal, holding a small white Spaniel, and her brother Bertie. This example is presented in white and gilt with flesh tones on the children's faces. The only other painted details are the children's hair and shoes. 9". Circa 1850. Value: $500.00-$550.00. *Courtesy of Anita L. Grashof, Gallerie Ani'tiques, Scotch Plains, NJ.*

The large red and white dog central to this composition is obviously a Setter but the small black and white puppy held by the young girl is a Spaniel. While combining dog-breeds in grouped figures was not the norm, the royal family combined several breeds in their household. The mold sculptor might have had that thought in mind when he created the design for this figure, and perhaps the girl in this piece is the Princess Royal holding her mother's favorite Spaniel, Dash, while her brother sits astride another family pet. 9". Circa 1850. Value: $725.00-$825.00. *Courtesy of Marla W. Chaikin, William Charles Antiques, Shrewsbury, NJ.*

This figure is characterized by a beauty of form often achieved by the so-called "simple" Staffordshire potters. Seated on a grassy hillock, the central figure of a young man holding a flute is perfectly balanced on the left and right by a Spaniel and a lamb. The symmetry is further enhanced by the placement of the man's elbows and knees. Although the presence of the lamb suggests that the young man might be a shepherd, the dog has no characteristics of any of the sheep-herding breeds. Incorporation of a Spaniel undoubtedly increased the market potential at a time when Spaniels were in vogue. 9". Circa 1850. Value: $550.00-$575.00. *Courtesy of Anita L. Grashof, Gallerie Ani'tiques, Scotch Plains, NJ.*

This large figure shows a kilted Scotsman whose right hand rests on a red and white Spaniel's head. Slip was used to highlight patches of scrub grass at the Scotsman's feet and to decorate the surface of the tree trunk beside him. A comprehensive color palette adds to the effective painted treatment of the human figure while simple coloring and a prominent red star on the Spaniel's back call attention to the dog's integral presence in the figure grouping. 15.25". Circa 1855. Value: $995.00-$1095.00. *Courtesy of Perry Joyce Antiques.*

A grassy seat, a leisurely pipe, a basket of flowers, and a Spaniel for company suggest the restful pleasures of a summer afternoon in rural England. Imaginative modeling, attention to detail, and an effective color palette are combined in this charming figure. 8". Circa 1855-1860. Value: $500.00-$575.00. *Author's Collection.*

This outstanding figure, in which a boy wearing knee breeches and boots balances a jug on his shoulder, is one of a pair. The boy stands beside a small spring and his Spaniel stands on hind legs, perhaps begging for a drink of water from the jug. 9". Circa 1860. Value: $1150.00-$1250.00 (for the pair). *Courtesy of Perry Joyce Antiques.*

A rare kennel grouping which portrays a young girl who has joined her pet on the roof of its house. An eye-pleasing pyramidal form has been combined with subtle molding, subdued painted decoration (except for the kennel door), and an intimation of child/pet companionship. 8.50". Circa 1860. Value: $575.00-$675.00 *Courtesy of Marla W. Chaikin, William Charles Antiques, Shrewsbury, NJ.*

The title of this impressively tall portrait figure appears in raised capitals on a white oval base. The Prince of Wales, as represented here, is dressed is a short jacket, neatly detailed waistcoat, and trousers. His right hand rests on a pink-draped pedestal and his left hand rests on a red and white Spaniel's head. It is probable that this figure was issued in 1862, along with several others, when the Prince's betrothal was announced. 14.50". Circa 1862. Value: $895.00-$1095.00. *Courtesy of Marla W. Chaikin, William Charles Antiques, Shrewsbury, NJ.*

These paired figures of children hugging their Spaniels while seated on the dogs' backs is a charming and heartwarming expression of the special relationship that exists between children and their dogs. 4". Circa 1865. Value: $895.00-$995.00. *Courtesy of Marla W. Chaikin, William Charles Antiques, Shrewsbury, NJ.*

A wistful-looking pair of miniature red and white Spaniels with gray-painted paws. Like many other mini-Spaniels, they wear collars and padlocks but no chains. 4.50". Circa 1845. Value: $525.00-$625.00. *Courtesy of Jane McClafferty, New Canaan, CT.*

This miniature red and white Spaniel was probably designed to serve as a ring holder. Its size suggests that it might have been intended to hold a child's rings. This early figure is extremely rare. 3.25". Circa 1845. Value: $375.00-$475.00. *Courtesy of Jane McClafferty, New Canaan, CT.*

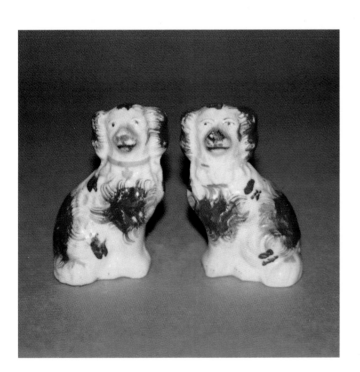

An early pair of red and white miniature Spaniel pups. 3". Circa 1845. Value: $395.00-$495.00. *Courtesy of Jane McClafferty, New Canaan, CT.*

Among the tiniest of the miniature Spaniels, this pup was purchased from a dealer in England who listed the figure as a salesman's sample. Its small size would have been suited to a salesman's carrying needs. Its extraordinary molded detail on both the front and the back and its carefully painted decoration would certainly have encouraged prospective buyers to purchase models of larger size. 2.50". Circa 1845-1850. Value: $325.00-$375.00. *Author's Collection.*

Back view showing the detailed molding on the salesman's sample shown in the preceding illustration. *Author's Collection.*

Small red and white Spaniel with an appealing upturned gaze. This little puppy is especially unique and lovely because it has a porcellaneous body. 4.50". Circa 1850. Value: $375.00-$475.00. *Author's Collection.*

This miniature black and white Spaniel is an example of early use of the sponge-painting technique. In this example the effect is light and lacy. The red-painted collar and padlock add an effective touch of contrast. 4.75". Circa 1845-1850. Value: $275.00-$375.00. *Courtesy of Anita L. Grashof, Gallerie Ani'tiques, Scotch Plains, NJ.*

A red and white mini-Spaniel which appears to be winking because one eye was left unpainted. 4". Circa 1850. Value: $250.00-$300.00. *Courtesy of Anita L. Grashof, Gallerie Ani'tiques, Scotch Plains, NJ.*

This small black and white Spaniel wears an orange collar and padlock; the feathered "bangs" are an unusual and charming touch. 5". Circa 1855. Value: $300.00-$400.00. *Courtesy of Nancy H. Furey.*

A diminutive red and white Spaniel seated on a footed quill holder cushion which is colored in cobalt blue and trimmed in gilt. 4". Circa 1855. Value: $385.00-$485.00. *Author's Collection.*

This debonair red and white miniature Spaniel wears a large feathered spot on its chest and a jaunty wisp of hair across its forehead. 3.75". Circa 1860. Value: $250.00-$350.00. *Courtesy of Jane McClafferty, New Canaan, CT.*

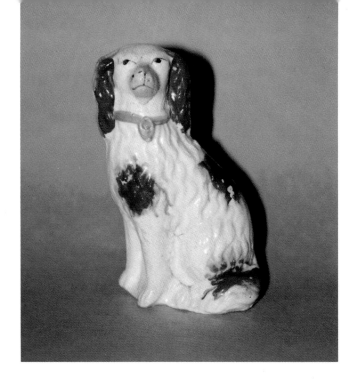

Red and white miniature Spaniel with a pale pink muzzle and red mouth. This is a common model sometimes seen in alternative coloring. 4.50". Circa 1870. Value: $250.00-$300.00. *Courtesy of Nancy H. Furey.*

Gold lustered miniature Spaniel with a pale pink nose and red mouth. 4.50". Circa 1870. Value: $250.00-$300.00. *Author's Collection.*

Miniature red and white Spaniel with a green collar and a band of green painted between the forelegs. 3.50". Circa 1875-1885. Value: $250.00-$300.00. *Author's Collection.*

Bottom view of the Spaniel shown in the preceding illustration. A small release hole is present; however, the bottom was not glazed. *Author's Collection.*

This copper lustered Spaniel is a perfect example of outstanding molding in miniature Spaniels. The body and one separately molded front leg were skillfully crafted with thoughtful attention to detail. The luster decoration is well-placed and applied with finesse. 5". Circa 1885-1890. Value: $325.00-$400.00. *Courtesy of Anita L. Grashof, Gallerie Ani'tiques, Scotch Plains, NJ.*

Miniature reproduction Dalmation, produced in porcelain and bearing an anchor mark in gold over the glaze. This mark was copied from a gold anchor found under the glaze on Chelsea porcelain. 3". Circa 1930-1950. Value: $35.00-$45.00. *Author's Collection.*

The gold anchor mark found on the Dalmation in the preceding illustration was applied on the top side of the base at the back of the figure. *Author's Collection.*

This miniature gold lustered reproduction Spaniel wears a neat little moustache and a somewhat quizzical expression. The figure was slip-cast with a completely open bottom. 3". Circa Mid-to-Late Twentieth Century. Value: $10.00-$12.00. *Courtesy of Jean A. Fromer, South Plainfield, NJ.*

These paired reproduction Spaniels are nearly identical to the single example shown in the preceding illustration except that the right-sided figure is a half inch taller and the gold spot on the left-sided figure is considerably larger. A paper sticker on the back of one of the figures states that the pair was manufactured in the U.S.A. Value for the pair: $20.00-$25.00. *Author's Collection.*

Paper sticker reading "Crown Stafford China, U.S.A." found glued to the back of one of the reproduction Spaniels shown in the preceding illustration. *Author's Collection.*

Novelty Spaniels

The idea of a jug or pitcher in the form of a Spaniel may seem a bit quirky but models of the sort illustrated here were popular among Victorian consumers whose taste for the ornamental was nothing if not fanciful. This novelty Spaniel jug was decorated in red and white with an artistically tied bow at the collar in place of the customary padlock. The handle was molded to provide a convenient and comfortable place for the thumb. All Spaniel jugs are considered rare. 8". Circa 1850. Value: $795.00-$895.00. *Courtesy of Perry Joyce Antiques.*

This familiar model was painted in red and white with a green bow at the collar. A slightly different look was achieved by the decorator who added thicker fur on the head, a wide center part, and a red line at the top. 8". Circa 1850. Value: $795.00-$895.00. *Courtesy of Marla W. Chaikin, William Charles Antiques, Shrewsbury, NJ.*

The cap on this exceptionally fine red and white begging Spaniel jug is decorated with purple grapes and green leaves, a decorating detail usually seen on jugs of this sort. Carefully placed patches of color appear on the "elbows" and "knees." 10.50". Circa 1850. Value: $1275.00-$1375.00. *Courtesy of Perry Joyce Antiques.*

Side view of the begging Spaniel shown in the preceding illustration. From this angle, the shape of the spout may be seen clearly, fitting nicely into a tricorn design, reminiscent of the tricorn, or cocked, hats once popular in Britain. *Courtesy of Perry Joyce Antiques.*

The red and white begging Spaniel portrayed in this novelty jug is wide-eyed, whimsical, and rare. 10.50". Circa 1850. Value: $1275.00-$1375.00. *Courtesy of Perry Joyce Antiques.*

Exquisite molding on this monochrome begging Spaniel jug is "crowned" by grapes and leaves. Sgraffito eyes and muzzle and a "studded" collar add to the uncompromised detail in this rare novelty figure. 10.25". Circa 1860-1870. Value: $1050.00-$1150.00. *Courtesy of Perry Joyce Antiques.*

One of the most popular Spaniel jug models is shown here colored in white and gilt, suggesting a production date after 1860. 7.50". Circa 1860-1870. Value: $700.00-$800.00. *Courtesy of Marla W. Chaikin, William Charles Antiques, Shrewsbury, NJ.*

A begging Spaniel jug decorated in white and gilt. 10". Circa 1860-1870. Value: $725.00-$825.00. *Author's Collection.*

What appears to be a severed head is actually a rare Spaniel bank with a coin slot cut into the back. Similar novelty Spaniels also appeared as tobacco jars and book ends. 5.50". Circa 1870. Value: $595.00-$695.00. *Courtesy of Jane McClafferty, New Canaan, CT.*

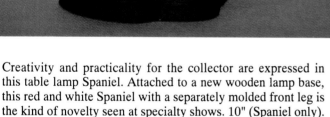

Creativity and practicality for the collector are expressed in this table lamp Spaniel. Attached to a new wooden lamp base, this red and white Spaniel with a separately molded front leg is the kind of novelty seen at specialty shows. 10" (Spaniel only). Circa 1870. Value: $525.00-$625.00. *Courtesy of Jane McClafferty, New Canaan, CT.*

These novelty book ends are certain attention-getters but they are not old. 5". Circa Twentieth Century. Value: $150.00-$175.00. *Courtesy of Marla W. Chaikin, William Charles Antiques, Shrewsbury, NJ.*

Novelty salt and pepper shakers, newly fashioned to mimic the original Staffordshire Spaniel character. 3.50". Circa 1950-1990. Value: $10.00-$20.00. *Author's Collection.*

This unusual-looking Spaniel appears to be sticking out its tongue. A new figure, it is completely unlike any reproduction previously recorded. Presented in stark white with no painted decoration, the Spaniel has been attached to a natural wood base. 10" (Spaniel only). Circa: Late Twentieth Century. Value: $100.00-$125.00. *Courtesy of Anita L. Grashof, Gallerie Ani'tiques, Scotch Plains, NJ.*

• G L O S S A R Y •

Bat — a sheet of wet clay; pressed into the sides of mold parts in the press-casting process used to pot Staffordshire Spaniels.

Best Gold — a powdered mercuric gold with a light, natural effect, used in gilding pottery products; the only gilding used to decorate Staffordshire Spaniel figures until circa 1860 when bright gold was introduced.

Beswick Pottery — pottery produced by a firm established in Longton by James Wright Beswick during the 1890s; the Beswick Pottery began producing animal statuary, including Spaniels, circa 1936.

Biscuit — a clay, earthenware, or porcelain object that has only been fired once and remains unglazed.

Body — a term used to denote the mixture of materials from which a pottery product is made (also called "paste.")

Bone China — a form of pottery composed of at least five per cent bone ash; not considered true porcelain.

Bow Factory — established during the 1740s in the ward of Stratford, England; produced a high-quality soft-paste porcelain that contains bone-ash; the factory closed in circa 1776.

Bright Gold — a liquid gilding with a brassy, mirror-like shine, used by the Staffordshire potters after 1860 and in many modern reproductions.

Ceramic — denotes wares composed of clay and fired at high temperatures.

Chelsea Porcelain and Derby Porcelain — Chelsea is a well-known and highly regarded soft-paste porcelain made at the Chelsea Factory in Chelsea, England (established circa 1745); the Chelsea Factory was bought-out by William Duesbury, of Crown Derby fame, in 1769 thus inaugurating the Chelsea-Derby period. A new Derby Factory was established in 1878 and is still in operation.

Cobalt Blue — a color made from an oxide of cobalt and used to decorate pottery products; popular during Victorian times and widely used in the decoration of Staffordshire figures.

Comforter Spaniels — a term used to denote Spaniel figures produced in Staffordshire during the nineteenth century; derives from Elizabethan times when ladies kept small Spaniels (called Spaniells Gentle) under their wide skirts to provide the "comfort" of added warmth during the cold winter months; the actual breed was probably a forerunner of the King Charles Spaniel and the Cavalier King Charles Spaniel; synonymous with Staffordshire Spaniels, Comforters, and Comforter Dogs.

Copper Luster — an iridescent metallic glaze used to decorate pottery wares; applied to a number of Staffordshire Spaniel figures; various lustered pottery products have been produced by applying to glazes metallic compounds that become iridescent films during firing.

Crazing — thin lines appearing on the glazed surface of a pottery product; caused by age and/or heat.

Creamware — a form of earthenware in which light colored clays from Devonshire were mixed with calcified flints to form a cream-colored pottery product; probably introduced by Thomas Astbury circa 1720 and refined by Josiah Wedgwood around 1740.

Earthenware — a form of pottery made from natural clays and fired at high temperatures; opaque, not vitreous, and possessing a porosity of over fifty per cent.

Embossing — a slightly raised pattern or design used to decorate a pottery product; formed from the clay paste before firing.

Enameling — a type of decorating in which enamel colors created from metallic oxides are applied over the glaze with which they fuse at low kiln temperatures; enamels were used to color some Spaniel figures.

Factory Marks — marks, either impressed, embossed, incised, transfer printed, or painted, on pottery products to identify the individual potter and/or pottery firm that produced the ware; nearly all authentic Staffordshire Spaniels were not marked, except for a certain few potted by Sampson Smith and John Lloyd.

Firing — baking clay items at high temperatures; firing may occur several times during different phases of the potting process.

Flux — a glassy material (i.e., feldspar, borax, bismuth) added to color bases to help them fuse with the glaze.

Gilding — a type of decoration using gold; gilding is common on the collars, padlocks, chains, and body finishing of many Spaniel types.

Glaze — a vitreous (liquid) or glassy substance applied to a pottery body in the biscuit state to make the ware impenetrable by fluids; glazes may be colored; during Victorian times, glazes were predominantly lead-glazes, although some salt-glazes were used.

Glost — synonymous with glaze; glazes were fired in glost-ovens.

Hard-Paste — porcelain fired at high temperatures and distinguished from soft-paste that has been fired at lower temperatures.

Impressed Factory Marks — words, numbers, symbols, etc. that are impressed into the body, usually the base, of a pottery product before firing as a means of identification; impressed marks are rare on Spaniel figures although mold numbers are seen from time to time; the rare impressed marks of Sampson Smith and John Lloyd appear on some Spaniel models.

Ironstone — a type of stoneware in which ground iron slag is mixed with clay; the English patent was established by James Mason in 1813.

Jackfield Ware — a type of pottery in which a black glaze is applied over red earthenware; the process for this type of pottery is generally believed to have originated in Jackfield, England, a town in Shropshire.

Kiln — an oven or chamber used to fire enameled pottery products, in Victorian times, usually made of brick in various sizes.

Mold — a form made from a sculptor's rendering in the shape desired for the final product; the mold holds the clay paste to give it form and molding detail; during the period of production associated with Staffordshire Spaniels, plaster of Paris molds were widely used; all Spaniels are molded figures.

Molding — the process by which a pottery product is given form; either by hand or in a prepared mold form.

Monochrome — objects that have been decorated with a single color; completely monochromed Spaniel figures are unusual as most are decorated with some color or gilt.

Motif — the central idea or theme of an object; in reference to Spaniel figures various motifs include flower basket, recumbent, novelty, grouped, etc.

Opacity — the quality of a body that makes it impervious to light; one cannot see through an opaque object; Staffordshire Spaniels are usually opaque.

Oven — a chamber larger than a kiln used to bring clay from the molded form to the biscuit or glost state.

Overglaze — decorative detail applied after a pottery product has been glazed and fired.

Portrait Figures — a classification of Staffordshire figures that refers to pottery representations of royal, historical, literary, mythical, and other persons; Staffordshire Spaniels are not considered portrait figures.

Paste — the clay body of a pottery product before it has been fired.

Plinth — the base or substructure of a pottery product; used synonymously with "base."

Porcelain — a fine translucent or semi-translucent ceramic, actually a form of stoneware fired to a state of vitrification, but distinguished from stoneware because of its translucence; usually made from kaolin, quartz, and feldspar; some Staffordshire Spaniels appear in porcellaneous form.

Pottery — all objects formed in clay and fired at high temperatures; the two main categories of pottery are earthenware and stoneware.

Press-Mold — a mold prepared from a sculptor's original model into which clay is pressed before decorating and firing; usually in two or more parts; most Staffordshire Spaniels were press-molded.

Quills and Quill Holders — quills are writing implements, used before pens were invented, either made from or designed to resemble the quills of feathers; quill holders are receptacles, often incorporated into pottery products, designed to hold quills.

Red Ware — unglazed red pottery sometimes known as Elers Ware, so named for John and David Elers; red wares, especially tea and coffee pots, were popular among the Staffordshire potters until approximately the second half of the eighteenth century.

Repairer — a highly skilled pottery worker responsible for repairing cracks, smoothing seams, assembling a figure or group from its mold parts, and otherwise repairing and refining wares.

Rococo — an eighteenth century style of design characterized by embellished patterns and curved spatial forms; relating to pottery, the term denotes ornately shaped wares; Rococo forms are found on several Spaniel bases but standard seated Spaniels do not appear with Rococo designs.

Salt-Glazing — a form of glazing used primarily during the eighteenth century in which wares were fired in a kiln to a high temperature at which time salt was added to form a hard, pitted glaze with a texture similar to that of an orange peel.

Sgraffito — a form of decoration produced, in pottery, by scratching through the surface of the pottery product.

Slip — a mixture of water and clay used in potting, primarily for decoration or for use in slip-molds.

Slip-Cast — a form of pottery-making in which slip is poured into a prepared mold, dried, and the excess slip mixture removed; slip-casting was rarely used in the production of period Staffordshire Spaniels but has been widely used in twentieth century reproductions.

Soft-Paste — a type of porcelain in which the ware is fired at a lower temperature than hard-paste porcelain; "soft" refers to the temperatures used and not to the texture of the ware.

Spills and Spill Vases — a spill is a long, rolled piece of paper used to light candles, oil lamps, and pipes from an already-existing fire source, common among families of modest means at a time when matches were expensive; spill vases are vase-like containers designed to hold paper spills and kept close to the hearth for easy access, often incorporated into Staffordshire pottery figures.

Staffordshire Pottery — a generic term applied to pottery products produced in the Staffordshire district of England, located 150 miles northwest of London.

Staffordshire Spaniels — an inclusive term assigned to Spaniel figures produced in abundance by the Staffordshire potters from roughly 1840 until 1890; representing the King Charles Spaniel and probably modeled after Queen Victoria's Spaniel "Dash;" standard Staffordshire Spaniels were potted in facing pairs intended to serve as mantlepiece ornaments; most are portrayed in a seated posture and appear in a wide range of colors and sizes; variant styles were also produced; synonymous with Comforter Spaniels, Comforter Dogs, and Comforters.

Stoneware — a classification of pottery, possessing an opacity of less than five per cent, that is fired at temperatures high enough to achieve vitrification.

Thénard's Blue — an underglaze cobalt color, developed by a French chemist named Thénard in 1802; popular and widely used on bases and in painted decoration during the early and mid-Victorian period of Staffordshire figure production; discontinued after 1863.

Translucency — the opposite of opacity; a chief characteristic of porcelain.

Underglaze — decoration applied to a pottery product before glazing and firing; most Spaniel figures were underglazed.

Vitreous — a glass-like quality achieved by glazes applied and fired onto pottery wares; stonewares and porcelains are vitreous because the body and glaze are fired in such a way that they become fused and impenetrable; earthenwares, fired at lower temperatures, may have vitreous or glass-like glazes but these can be penetrated (thus resulting in crazing).

Wedgwood — the most famous of the Staffordshire pottery families potting during the eighteenth and nineteenth centuries; Wedgwood wares are world-known and have been widely copied and imitated; particularly noted are creamware products and Jasper Wares.

• C O N C L U S I O N •

Although Staffordshire Spaniels were produced in the hundreds of thousands, substantially large numbers have been lost or broken during the past one hundred and fifty years. Most Spaniel pairs were not treated as prospective heirlooms. They were not placed in special cabinets and kept untouched for generations as was the case with their fine china and porcelain contemporaries.

Spaniels "lived" humble lives in humble homes. They collected dust and ash from the fireplaces they decorated, and they were subject to all the nicks and chips of daily life in cottage households. They were exposed to the chill of winter nights and the heat of blazing fires. Children undoubtedly played with them. Although they were not a practical possession, they did experience a lot of daily "wear."

By the end of the nineteenth century, styles and tastes had begun to change. The Potteries, along with other British industries, needed to accommodate consumer demand for the fresh and the new. Spaniel production continued but not in the great numbers it once had and by the time of World War I, Spaniels had become, more or less, passé.

For several decades, the Comforter's modest origins and absorbing history (including the poignant fact of child labor) did little to spark the collector's or the "antique hound's" interest. The Spaniel's soulful expression and bulky body did not place it among the most highly prized Staffordshire wares. For a long time, it seemed as if Comforter Spaniels were too commonplace, too plentiful, and they became the "underdogs" of Staffordshire collecting, largely overlooked in favor of other canine statuary, portrait figure studies, and older Staffordshire products.

In recent years, however, Comforter Spaniels have enjoyed a renewed popularity. As their numbers have decreased, and models in mint or near-mint condition have become increasingly difficult to find, collector interest has surged. Spaniels are currently commanding prices far greater than their potters might ever have imagined. Pairs which sold for a few pennies in 1840 are now selling at better auctions and shows for a thousand dollars and more (sometimes much more!).

Like other Victorian collectibles, Staffordshire Spaniels have become older and have thus gained a more credible antique status. Collectors generally collect because the object they seek is aesthetically pleasing, because collecting that item presents a challenge and provides a sense of the "treasure hunt," because the subject of their collection is not generally available, or because that item has become trendy. In other words, collectors become interested in a particular item because it is old, beautiful, rare, or fashionable to collect. This is certainly the case with Staffordshire Spaniels, and it is safe to assume that their growing value will never depreciate.

The art and history conscious sensibilities of today's collectors have greatly impacted the high regard in which Staffordshire Spaniels are currently held. Additionally, and importantly, it seems that most Spaniel collectors experience a profound affective response to the dogs they collect. These collectors recognize a sound investment with future growth potential but there is as much of the heart as there is of the wallet in their quest.

Perhaps the most subjective factor in the Spaniel's return to popularity is that each seemingly naive-but-knowing Comforter reminds us of an era which, despite its flaws, was romantic and picturesque — a era long past but not yet lost on the moors of time.

Opposite page.

Although pottery Spaniels were all the rage during the nineteenth century, they were not usually treated with special care. Most were not locked away in special cabinets, nor were they regarded as prospective heirlooms. Today, however, Spaniels are a treasured collectible, displayed in cases and cabinets and on specially-built shelves by private collectors, and antique dealers, throughout the world. *Courtesy of Marla W. Chaikin, William Charles Antiques, Shrewsbury, NJ.*

This papier-mâché Spaniel was purchased in a large department store early in 1996 and illustrates how popular the Staffordshire Spaniel "look" has become again, a century and a half after it was first introduced. *Author's Collection.*

• ENDNOTES •

INTRODUCTION

1. Kenyon Kies, *Collecting Victorian Staffordshire Pottery Figures* (1989), 10.
2. David Sekers, *Popular Staffordshire Pottery* (1977), 11.
3. Kies, 10, 12.

CHAPTER 1

1. Clive Mason Pope, *A-Z of Staffordshire Dogs, A Potted History* (1990), 6.
2. ibid.
3. ibid.
4. ibid.
5. ibid.
6. ibid.
7. ibid.
8. ibid, 7.
9. ibid, 72.
10. ibid.

CHAPTER 2

1. P. D. Gordon Pugh, *Staffordshire Portrait Figures of the Victorian Era* (1987), 17.
2. Petra Williams, *Flow Blue China, An Aid to Identification*, (Introduction) "A Simplified History of the Making of Pottery In Staffordshire, England" (1971), 1.
3. ibid.
4. ibid.
5. ibid.
6. ibid, 2.
7. Kenyon Kies, *Collecting Victorian Staffordshire Pottery Figures* (1989), 7.
8. Geoffrey Godden, *An Illustrated Encyclopedia of British Pottery and Porcelain* (1966), xv.
9. ibid, 2.
10. ibid.
11. ibid.
12. Kies, 30.
13. Williams, 3.
14. Pugh, 17-31.
15. Kies, 8, 47-48 and Pugh, 17-31.
16. Kies, 18.

CHAPTER 3

1. Kenyon Kies, *Collecting Victorian Staffordshire Pottery Figures* (1989), 8.
2. ibid.
3. ibid, 8, 10.
4. P. D. Gordon Pugh, *Staffordshire Portrait Figures of the Victorian Era* (1987), 87.
5. ibid.
6. Kies, 10.
7. Pugh, 87.
8. Kies, 10 and Pugh, 87-88.
9. Pugh, 88.

CHAPTER 4

1. Kenyon Kies, *Collecting Victorian Staffordshire Pottery Figures* (1989), 10.
2. Anita Grashof (Gallerie Ani'tiques), personal communication, 1996.
3. Kies, 10.
4. P. D. Gordon Pugh, *Staffordshire Portrait Figures of the Victorian Era* (1987), 88.
5. ibid.
6. ibid.
7. ibid.
8. ibid.
9. Kies, 38; Pugh, 88-89; and Clive Mason Pope, *A-Z of Staffordshire Dogs* (1990), 143.
10. Ralph and Terry Kovel, *Kovels' Know Your Antiques* (1981), 15-17.

CHAPTER 5

1. Clive Mason Pope, *A-Z of Staffordshire Dogs* (1990), 11.
2. Anita Grashof (Gallerie Ani'tiques), personal communication, 1995.
3. Pope, 74 and Kenyon Kies, *Collecting Victorian Staffordshire Pottery Figures* (1989), 4.
4. Kies, 4.
5. Pope, 110.
6. ibid, 106.
7. ibid, 100.
8. Geoffrey Godden, *An Illustrated Encyclopedia of British Pottery and Porcelain* (1996), xiv.

9. Pope, 92.
10. ibid, 130.
11. *Shroeder's Antiques Price Guide*, edited by Sharon and Bob Huxford, (1990), 50.

CHAPTER 6

1. Clive Mason Pope, *A-Z of Staffordshire Dogs* (1990), 86.
2. ibid.

CHAPTER 7

1. P. D. Gordon Pugh, *Staffordshire Portrait Figures of the Victorian Era* (1987), 98-103.
2. ibid, 24.
3. Kenyon Kies, *Collecting Victorian Staffordshire Pottery Figures*, (1989), 37.

CHAPTER 8

1. Kenyon Kies, *Collecting Victorian Staffordshire Pottery Figures* (1989), 37.
2. Anita Grashof (Gallerie Ani'tiques), personal communication, 1995.
3. *Antique & Collector's Reproduction News*, "On the Trail of Staffordshire Dogs," Feb. 1995, Vol. 4, #2, 16.
4. ibid, 16-17.
5. P. D. Gordon Pugh, *Staffordshire Portrait Figures of the Victorian Era* (1987), 103.
6. *Antique & Collectors Reproduction News*, 16.
7. ibid.
8. Kies, 37.
9. *Antique & Collectors Reproduction News*, 18.
10. ibid.
11. Kies, 38, 40.
12. *Antique & Collectors Reproduction News*, 24.
13. ibid.
14. ibid.

• *BIBLIOGRAPHY* •

Antique & Collectors Reproduction News. "New Staffordshire Figures from China," July 1996, Vol. 5, #7.

_____. "On the Trail of Staffordshire Dogs," February 1995, Vol. 4, #2.

Balston, Thomas. *Staffordshire Portrait Figures of the Victorian Age*. London: Faber & Faber, Ltd., 1958.

_____. *Supplement to Staffordshire Portrait Figures of the Victorian Age*. London: John Hall, 1963.

Bedford, John. *Staffordshire Pottery Figures*. New York: Walker & Walker, 1964.

Cushion, J.P. *English China Collecting for Amateurs*. London: Frederick Muller, 1967.

Dickens, Charles. *Oliver Twist*. New York: Simon & Schuster, Inc. (Pocket Books), 1957.

Godden, Geoffrey A., F.R.S.A. *An Illustrated Encyclopedia of British Pottery and Porcelain*. New York: Crown Publishing, 1966.

_____. *British Pottery and Porcelain 1780-1850*. London: Arthur Barker, Ltd., 1963.

_____. *The Concise Guide to British Pottery and Porcelain*. London: Barrie & Jenkins, 1990.

Gohm, Douglas. *Small Antiques for the Collector*. New York: Arco Publishing Co., 1968.

Grashof, Anita (Gallerie Ani'tiques), personal communications, Scotch Plains, New Jersey, 1995 & 1996.

Haggar, Reginald. *Staffordshire Chimney Ornaments*. London: Phoenix House, Ltd., 1955.

Honey, W. B. *English Pottery & Porcelain*. London: Adam & Charles Black, 1962 [new edition of 1933 original].

Hughes, Bernard and Therle. *The Collector's Encyclopaedia of English Ceramics*. London: Abbey Library, 1968.

Hughes, G. B. *English Pottery and Porcelain Figures*. New York: Praeger, 1968.

Kies, Kenyon Charles. *Collecting Victorian Staffordshire Pottery Figures*. 1989.

Kovel, Ralph and Terry. *Kovels' Know Your Antiques*. New York: Crown Publishers, Inc., 1981.

_____. *Kovels' New Dictionary of Marks. Pottery & Porcelain, 1850 to the Present*. New York: Crown Publishers, 1986.

Kowalsky, Arnold, personal communications, Yonkers, New York, 1996.

Lewis, Griselda. *Collector's History of English Pottery*. London: Studio Vista, 1969 and New York: Viking Press, 1969.

McClafferty, Jane (Jane McClafferty Antiques), personal communications, New Canaan, Connecticut, 1995 & 1996.

Morley-Fletcher, Hugo. *Investing in Pottery and Porcelain*. New York: Clarkson N. Potter, Inc., 1968.

Oliver, Anthony. *Staffordshire Pottery, The Tribal Art of England*. London: Heinemann, 1981.

_____. "Victorian Staffordshire Pottery Animals," *The Antiques Dealer and Collectors Guide*, January, 1971, p. 82.

Pope, Clive Mason. *A-Z of Staffordshire Dogs A Potted History*. Oxon, England: Classic Press, 1990.

Pugh, P. D. Gordon. *Staffordshire Portrait Figures of the Victorian Era*. Suffolk, England: Antique Collectors' Club (revised edition), 1987.

Sekers, David. *Popular Staffordshire Pottery*. London: Michael Joseph, Ltd., 1977.

Shroeder's Antiques Price Guides, edited by Sharon and Bob Huxford. Paducah, Kentucky: Collector's Books, 1990-1996.

Stanley, Louis T. *Collecting Staffordshire Pottery*. London: W. H. Allen, 1963.

Wakefield, Hugh. *Victorian Pottery*. New York: Universe Books, 1970.

Williams, Petra. "A Simplified History of the Making of Pottery in Staffordshire, England" (introduction), *Flow Blue China, An Aid to Identification*. Jeffersontown, Kentucky: Fountain House East, 1971.

• INDEX •